THE LITTLE BOOK OF
NONPROFIT LEADERSHIP

AN EXECUTIVE DIRECTOR'S HANDBOOK FOR
SMALL (AND VERY SMALL) NONPROFITS

ERIK HANBERG

For my dad

CONTENTS

INTRODUCTION

Welcome to the exciting world of nonprofit leadership! Where there's a new fire every day just begging to be put out, and everyone needs something from you. Right now.

What's new today? Well, your board needs your revisions on the next meeting agenda. And your bookkeeper needs an hour of your time to review some expenses. Oh, and one of your volunteers just caused a small flood in the kitchen and needs a mop.

(Why are you doing this again?)

Well, I'll tell you. Because the world needs you to step up and make your nonprofit the best it can be.

So *please* don't despair.

Use this book to get a handle on your organization and find the levers that will help you start leading change both in your organization and in your community.

Let's get started together.

Who this book is for

When I first was hired to run a nonprofit—the Grand Cinema in my hometown of Tacoma, Washington—I was all of twenty-three years old. The stars had aligned for me to get this job. I knew the board chair because she had seen my work at another nonprofit. I had also been a volunteer at the Grand for more than a year. Like the other volunteers, I signed up for shifts taking tickets, sweeping theaters, and making popcorn, which meant that I knew the organization but at the same time I wasn't *too* close. And the final star to align was that my job at another nonprofit had a tangential relationship to the world of film (in my job in economic development, I was nominally the "film commissioner" for Tacoma, which meant that every so often I tried to help movie studios find locations in the Tacoma area that would be good for filming). It wasn't a big deal, but it looked pretty good on the résumé when I was applying to run a nonprofit movie theater!

I also worked my butt off to prepare for the interview, I should add. It was an intense interview process, capped by interviewing in front of the full board of seventeen.

I got the job—managing director of the Grand Cinema. When the local movie reviewer called me up to interview me about the new position, he asked how old I was. I hedged and said, "I'll be twenty-four next month." To which he answered in his wonderful deadpan manner, "So you're twenty-three."

Yes. Yes, I was twenty-three, about to take on the responsibility of running a nonprofit with a $650,000 budget at the time.

I'm in my forties now with plenty of gray in my beard, and —in many ways—I'm writing this book for twenty-three-year-old Erik, who had a love of film and a lot of tenacity, but was totally new to what it meant to actually run a nonprofit. Which means that I'm also writing it for the thousands and thousands of nonprofit leaders out there who come to this work by following their passion but soon find they suddenly need a whole new set of skills to manage a nonprofit.

Maybe you have just been hired, but haven't actually started working at your nonprofit, and this book is a crash course in how to be an Executive Director (ED). Or maybe you have been at an organization for a couple years but are finding that nothing seems to be changing and the organization isn't progressing as you feel it should be.

Whether you are new to the job or just want a fresh start, this book is for you.

My story

As mentioned above, my first job as the director of a nonprofit was at twenty-three. The Grand Cinema was (and is) a nonprofit theater in downtown Tacoma. Leading the organization was something of a dream job for a film buff like me, but the position also cemented my love for working in and with nonprofits.

Later, I was the Executive Director of City Club of Tacoma, a nonpartisan nonprofit that focused on civic dialogue in our community. Later still, I helped out two nonprofits as Interim Executive Director for a few months at each organization. One was focused on youth and the other was the local chapter of the Audubon Society.

In between those times, I've served at nonprofits in positions of marketing and fundraising, including work in economic development, public radio, and education. Additionally, for eleven years my wife and I ran a small business together called Side x Side Creative, which helped nonprofits with their marketing and branding. I also have four books (counting this one) for nonprofit leaders, which has opened up opportunities for me to consult with dozens of other nonprofit organizations around the US and Canada.

And finally, I've sat on more than a dozen boards and committees and have served in locally elected office for more than eleven years, so I also bring a strong understanding of the governance side of an organization as well.

In other words, I really like nonprofits and have been drawn to this work for the last twenty years.

My books are all tailored to "small (and very small) nonprofits." I actually have a lot of experience at both small and large organizations. But there is a reason I focus my work on small nonprofits. The first is the most basic—small nonprofit leaders need the most help. Their staff are the most likely to be undertrained and new to the job. (I'm writing to the young me, remember?) They try to copy what they see the big nonprofits do, but they often ape the wrong things. This is how tiny nonprofits kill themselves trying to throw an over-the-top gala, not realizing that the hospital gala they were inspired to mimic has a full-time person planning it year-round. One of my goals for this book, and for all my books for small nonprofits, is to help you understand what the big guys are doing that will actually work for a small nonprofit like yours and to help you avoid the things that only work at larger organizations.

I also write for small nonprofit leaders because they are in the place to do the most good. If we can get our small nonprofits working better, we can really make a difference. The head of a nonprofit with three offices scattered across the state doesn't need my help as much as the scrappy environmental nonprofit restoring a salmon-bearing stream.

I also have chosen to write for leaders of small nonprofits because I know that these small nonprofit EDs have read other books on nonprofits and found themselves excluded by the traditional nonprofit literature. When a book recommends delegating a project to your Vice President of Human Resources, and you don't have one (or anything close to it), what do you do then? When a book weighs the pros and cons of whether you should have one, two, or several major gift officers, and you don't have any dedicated development staff, let alone a major gifts officer, you have to work hard to draw the parallels to your own organization. So let's switch it up. The big guys are welcome to stay, but they will have to be the ones extrapolating this time.

(That said, I distinctly remember walking into the office of an Executive Director of a twenty-million-dollar organization and seeing my book on fundraising on his shelf. It made me happy to know that even though I'm writing to such a specific audience, there was enough there to be useful to someone like him.)

What is a small nonprofit?

At some point during this section, you might have wondered, "Well, just how big is a small nonprofit anyway?" In general, I think small nonprofits have budgets under a million dollars a year, though usually they are in the "few hundred thousand dollars" range. Very small nonprofits usually have budgets that are less than one hundred thousand and often no staff (or just one additional staff member).

But let's not get caught up on the numbers, because that can vary among organizations and geographies. Small nonprofits usually don't have many levels of hierarchies—not much separates the ED from the front-line staff. They usually have small "working boards" without a big "name" on them. And they are full of passionate people—both staff and volunteers—who are there because they love the mission. Does that sound like your organization? I bet it does.

Meet Linda

In my experience the best way to teach something is through stories. To avoid the need for me to lecture you the whole time, we're going to follow an Executive Director of a fictional nonprofit and follow her journey through the trials and tribulations that are nearly universal to managers and leaders of small nonprofits.

With that in mind, let me introduce you to Linda. Linda is the Executive Director of the Smallville Historical Society. The small nonprofit has a state contract to operate a pioneer cabin in Smallville. They also earn a little bit of revenue from memberships, donations, educational programming, and merchandise sales. But the bulk of the revenue comes from that state contract.

Linda doesn't necessarily have a strong affinity to the pioneer cabin, per se. But she likes history in general and she loves the history of Smallville. In fact, she loves everything about her hometown. She has an encyclopedic knowledge of Smallville and its history and she loves having a job that lets her live in that world full-time.

We'll follow Linda's path as an Executive Director, with many stops along the way for commentary, points, and counterpoints by yours truly.

Onward

Let's jump into Linda's time at the Smallville Historical Society! She's about to learn just what the job of an ED actually entails.

PART ONE
MISSION, PEOPLE, MONEY

GETTING YOUR HEAD AROUND YOUR NONPROFIT

ONE

WHAT DOES AN EXECUTIVE DIRECTOR ACTUALLY DO?

WHY DID the board of directors hire you?

And to be clear, I mean *you* specifically, the Executive Director of your nonprofit. Can you name it? Is it because you connect really well with donors? Because you are a master of logistics? Because your love of community theater is infectious? Because you know how to scale a rapidly growing organization? Because the nonprofit has never had an ED before and they are looking to you for guidance on how this whole thing is supposed to work?

Every nonprofit hires its leader for a different reason. It changes between nonprofits and it will change over time within the same nonprofit. The ED of a young nonprofit may just be trying to keep the doors open. The next ED may cement programming. The next, fundraising. The next will lead a broadening of the scope of the mission to include the entire state. And the next may have to pull back some of those ambitions in order to keep the doors open, just like the first ED!

Some Executive Directors can grow with a single organization through all these phases. And others will find that they like certain phases more than others. So they will look outside of any particular mission and excel at leading different kinds of organizations through similar periods of their history. Some EDs are great at whipping large bureaucracies into shape, others love taking fledgling organizations and giving them the marketing support they deserve to make them shine like rock stars. Still others love the thrill of a nonprofit's first capital campaign.

There's no right answer. What are *you* here for?

———

Linda, at the Smallville Historical Society, was starting to ask herself that very question. Every fall and spring, the pioneer cabin was overrun with school groups. She had just finished yet another tour and she was exhausted. She wasn't used to working with so many kids so many days a week. It drained her.

Before becoming the Smallville Historical Society's Executive Director, her previous work experience had been at an insurance company. After several years there, she took a break from work to raise her kids, and during that time came to really love the Smallville Historical Society. She visited the pioneer cabin when her kids were young, and when they were older, she remained a donor at the Historical Society. When the founding Executive Director announced his retirement, Linda decided to throw her hat in the ring. And she got the job!

It was a great title for her and came with real responsibility (even if the pay was much lower than she had earned at the insurance company). But it was flexible work and for an organization she loved.

But now that it was her one-year anniversary as the Executive Director, the bloom was off the rose.

The job just didn't feel very good anymore. What had gone wrong?

She looked back at the last year. She had started with so many big ideas...but nothing had truly advanced. In addition to the school tours and all the time they took, the difficulties of handling board members and the small staff were starting to weigh on her. The pioneer cabin itself seemed to need constant maintenance. And she was always being called to put out (metaphorical) fires, so her days kept getting away from her, no matter how well she planned ahead. She joked that she was "chief cook and bottle washer," but lately it seemed like she was mostly washing bottles—with no one at the stove cooking. Worst of all, she used to love history, but now she just wasn't connecting with the mission anymore.

Linda took a rare personal day and went to a lake outside of Smallville. She got out a piece of paper and started writing. The first thing she wrote: What is my job?

She wrote and she wrote. Was leading school tours of the cabin and grounds her job? If she looked at it in terms of hours spent, the tours were clearly a big part of her job in the fall and spring. She scheduled all the tours, which often took a lot of email and phone time, and she led every one. And after the students left, she cleaned up and had to enter the data from the tour into a mandatory statewide website that was a part of her contract with the state. Add it all up, and she figured that every time there was a tour, it took half a day away from other things she could be doing. During the spring and the fall there were a couple tours every week, sometimes more. So it was definitely a big part of her job.

But when she looked at it from other angles, calling those tours her job didn't feel right. Most of the tasks related to the tours weren't on her official job description, for one. And, when it came right down to it, she dreamt of hiring someone else to take over the work. So was it actually her job if she could just hire someone else to do it? It was what she *did*, yes.

Where she spent her time. But it also wasn't quite her job either.

That gave her a sense of relief, because it had been starting to feel like she was trapped into doing school tours forever. But just as she started to feel like a burden was being lifted from her shoulders, she had another thought: whether she liked it or not, she was responsible for everything. If something went wrong with the school tours, the board would look to her, even if it wasn't technically her "job."

"Well, fine," she said aloud. "I'm tired of doing the tours but I'm always going to have to be responsible for them in the end. So maybe there's another way to make them happen."

Now she did a lot more focused writing and brainstorming. After a while, she called her board president.

"Linda," he greeted her. "I thought you were taking a personal day?"

"I am. And I've been doing a lot of thinking. I need someone to take over school tours for me."

The board president was quiet for a moment. "Ah. Well... I'm sure they are a ton of work. But I have to ask, do we have the money for that?"

"No," Linda answered quietly. "Or at least, I don't think so. I don't know for sure. But I have to be honest with you. The tours are killing me. I don't get anything else done when they're here. And in the spring and fall, it seems like it's all I do."

"I hope this is clear, Linda: we don't want to lose you," he said. "So we will do whatever we can."

"Oh!" Linda exclaimed. "I'm not threatening to leave. I'm just—"

"You're just burnt out. I get it. And I know you're not threatening. But if you're feeling like this after your first year, you're not going to stay long. So let's figure out what we can do."

"I only have a handful of tours left this spring. Then I get a break until they pick up again in September. I'd love to start the next school year with something new in place. So that gives me...four months to figure it out."

"Four months. I'm sure we can do it," he answered. "Let me know what I can do to help."

They said goodbye and Linda hung up the phone.

Now she was actually feeling better. She decided to take a walk around the lake and enjoy the beautiful spring day.

So what had changed? She had just given herself a massive new project! Why did that make Linda feel better?

Working *on* your nonprofit versus working *in* your nonprofit

The most important thing that had changed was Linda's frame of mind. Up until that point, she had been doing the work of the nonprofit. But now she was working *on* the nonprofit itself. She was embarking on a project that would change the way work happened at the organization. It would improve both her daily life and—if she could successfully implement it—she would improve the nonprofit itself. She was now thinking about the organization as an entity outside of her regular job and trying to make it better, as opposed to just doing the tasks that had always been done.

Linda had just grasped a key insight: If you only do the day-to-day tasks of your nonprofit, you (and the nonprofit) will never get anywhere. You have to change how you actually go about the work. Figuring out what that means for your nonprofit is the most important job of the Executive Director.

Being a leader versus being an employee

I'm going to linger here for a moment because I believe it's crucial that we talk about the Executive Director's job to step above the fray. I wrote above that Linda had changed her mentality: no longer was she working *in* her nonprofit, now she was working *on* it. But another mental shift had happened as well—she wasn't thinking like an employee of the nonprofit anymore. She was thinking like a leader.

If you have had a lot of prior work experience as an employee and are new to a leadership or management role, this can be a hard shift, so it's worth teasing out what I mean by it.

Linda the employee accepted that she needed to lead all the school tours because that's what the last Executive Director did. She grumbled about it, certainly, and wished she could change it, but she never actually did anything about it.

Whereas Linda the leader finally decided that her time was better spent doing something else, and so she took an active step toward making it happen. She sketched some ideas out and she called her board president to start the ball rolling.

There is a lot more to leadership than just making an active step toward changing an organization. But as a distinguishing difference between a leader and an employee, it's a pretty good indicator—did you actually work to make something different and better (a leader) or did you sit back and take what was given, even if you thought there could be a better way (an employee)?

As an aside, I want to be clear about something: the best employees think like leaders. An employee who thinks of ways to improve the business or nonprofit as a whole (and takes active steps to make it happen) is incredibly valuable.

But the reverse—leaders who think like employees—can get a nonprofit stuck in a rut very quickly.

Decisions versus hours

I want to propose a thought experiment to further explore this mental mindset that Executive Directors should strive for.

Imagine an Executive Director who appears to be a "slacker." She just doesn't seem to be working very hard. She comes in at 9:30. She leaves at 3:30. She isn't very good at replying to emails or returning phone calls. But over the course of a year, she just nails three really key decisions. I mean really *nails* them.

Now imagine a very, very busy Executive Director. She is in the office at 6:00 a.m. and leaves at 6:00 p.m. She is a flurry of activity. She's on the phone, she's scheduling meetings over coffee, she's always working and always busy. She's so busy, in fact, that she just misses that there were even three key decisions to make. Those opportunities pass right by her and the nonprofit.

Certainly, something useful is happening at the busy ED's nonprofit—you can't work sixty hours a week and have *nothing* happen. But I think there is a strong case to be made that, over a period of a couple years, the nonprofit run by the supposedly slacker ED will start to do better than the nonprofit run by the busy ED. Not *because* she's a slacker, certainly, but because she recognizes decision points and she makes the right call. (*Please* don't read this as me giving permission to put in the bare minimum at your job. Making good decisions usually comes from your experience and knowing your organization and your community deeply. Those two things take time and energy.)

The larger point stands: your success at the nonprofit is primarily about recognizing decisions and getting them (mostly) right. Whether they are big decisions or little ones, whether they are snap decisions or the result of a complex process in partnership with the board, decision-making is at the core of your job as an Executive Director.

I'll link this to the "leader versus the employee" mindset. An employee tries to show her value by how much she works. Linda the employee could have told the board, "Look how much I'm working on school tours for you. Look how committed I am. There are so many tours, and they are so much work, but I'm doing them and I'm doing them really well." In essence: "Look how much you need me."

Whereas leaders show their value through their decisions. Linda the leader said, "School tours are taking up too much of my time, time that could be going to fundraising, program building, or other important work. I'm going to come up with some ideas to make this work better for the nonprofit."

Managing operations

Deciding who runs the school tours is not up to the board. It's up to Linda, the ED. The Executive Director is in charge of making sure the work of the nonprofit gets done, however that's defined, on behalf of the board. *How* that happens, though, shouldn't be up to the board. It's best left to the expertise of the ED, who should know better than anyone else how to go about actually doing the work.

That means sometimes the ED delegates certain tasks and jobs to staff, to volunteers, or maybe even (in very small nonprofits) to board members who are willing to do the work of the nonprofit under the supervision of the Executive Director.

And, of course, the ED can do the work of the nonprofit herself. The smaller the nonprofit, the more common this is. However it is handled, who does what and how they do it is the decision of the Executive Director. An ED should keep the board informed, as Linda did, but it's her call.

The board's employee

And yet, for all of that, I now have to address a key truth: the Executive Director *is* an employee of the nonprofit's board and works within their guidelines.

But it's a strange relationship. The Executive Director doesn't really have a single boss, but rather a group of people who can make employment decisions about her. The board members don't work on-site with their employee either, even though they supervise her. The employee is paid for her work, but the board members are not. And, despite being her "supervisors," the board relies on her for knowledge and expertise about the organization. After all, she is living the mission every day, while the board is not.

It's an unusual relationship in the employment world.

I have another book (*The Little Book of Boards*) that really dives deep into the board's role and how to be a good board member, but I will sum up a board's key responsibilities in brief here. A good board:

- ensures that the organization is living up to its mission
- oversees finances and budgeting
- sets policy
- leads long-term planning
- fundraises
- "hires and fires" the Executive Director
- improves itself

What's missing from this list? *Telling the Executive Director what to do.*

The board sets guidelines, through its policies and through

its budget, but within those, the operational decisions are up to the Executive Director.

An ED who turns to the board for direction on operational decisions is abdicating her responsibility and miring the board in tasks that should not be on their plate. Because boards will often eagerly take an ED up on the offer! Board members frequently *want* to be doing operations. They love the nonprofit and the work they do. So an ED who turns to the board for these things will often find a waiting audience. But the time they spend critiquing a brochure, or digging into a nonprofit's program, is time that they aren't spending doing the rest of their core functions.

So my call to Executive Directors is this: leading the organization means also leading the board. It's more delicate because you are leading your own bosses, but it's important. I'll dive a lot more into the ED/board relationship later in this book to investigate how it works.

Can you get out of daily operations of your nonprofit?

Now that I've said that an ED is responsible for operations, my next challenge to you is this: Can you get yourself out of the daily operations of your nonprofit? Of course, you will always be involved to some extent. But what would it take for the organization to not be reliant on you every moment of the day? That's what I'm talking about here.

The smaller your nonprofit, the harder this will be. But here's the truth: the more you can extricate yourself from the daily operations of your nonprofit, the more the real work of your job can begin. For the ED of a very small nonprofit, this might only be a few hours a week. For a leader of a nonprofit with a handful of staff members, there might be more opportunity to make time for this.

I experienced this firsthand at the Grand Cinema. The person who had been in the position before me was integral to the daily operations of the movie theater. When I was hired, the board said (essentially) that they'd like me to do everything he did, plus fundraising, plus creating new special events, plus new educational programs. That's a lot of new things to do! I realized very quickly that I had to reshape the organization in a way that my job was not essential to its daily operations. I delegated many tasks that the previous manager used to do. Some jobs he did I was even able to address with small capital improvements. I streamlined other procedures using technology. And finally, for some duties I simply changed how I approached them to make them easier on myself.

There wasn't any one decision that changed my relationship to the operations of the theater. But over time, they added up. Two years after I started, I was swamped with a special event—the largest one I had attempted to date. In the midst of planning it, I realized that I had barely been involved with the daily operations of the theater for the last two weeks. The system was working, and I could spend my time pushing us forward into new places.

It might sound scary—like you are "working yourself out of a job." But the more the daily operations of your nonprofit can do without you, the better you will be able to lead.

Systems beat caring

Getting out of the daily work of the nonprofit often means delegating, but sometimes it means figuring out the checklist for any given action and turning it into an easily repeatable routine—something that doesn't take a lot of your thought process anymore, but that still makes sure it happens.

For example, let's say that part of the regular operations of the nonprofit is to post a monthly schedule of events in the front window. This is exactly the kind of thing that an overworked Executive Director can let slip through the cracks. It becomes a source of guilt and shame when the ED notices every morning in May that the poster window still has March's events. And yet she still never manages to get to it! The shame compounds.

If you don't have anyone to delegate the work to, the next best option is to create a system. Try setting a recurring reminder on the last day of each month to change the poster. Either on your calendar or a trusted to-do app. It will become routine, and part of a checklist of regular things that have to happen. The more you offload these into small tasks like this, the easier it is to just simply do them.

I have taken this idea to an extreme in my work today. I have recurring weekly, monthly, quarterly, and annual reminders for a variety of tasks. I have weekly reminders to go through my inbox, monthly reminders to ask people for certain information, quarterly reminders for certain big-picture projects that I want to keep top of mind, and even annual reminders for small things I need to do every year that would easily slip through the cracks otherwise.

You don't have to take it to that level to get use out of this. When you turn the day-to-day tasks into easily repeatable jobs, you're less likely to stress about them while also making sure they get done. *And*, it's easier to eventually hire for them, because the job is right there in the task list!

I've heard this concept phrased another way. The sculptor Elizabeth King says, "Process saves us from the poverty of our intentions." This really resonates with me. Don't trust yourself to simply just *care* enough to replace the poster in the window. Some months there will just be other things to do and you'll forget. Or you will get overwhelmed by all the daily tasks you are caring so much about that you are spending sixty hours a week doing them, while still not actually leading the organization.

Systems beat caring. Process beats intention. Get as much of these sorts of things out of your brain and onto paper or into a computer. Future You will thank you.

I have a special bonus chapter on time management, productivity, calendars, and more that are specifically tailored to the ED of a small nonprofit. Download it at http://bit.ly/LBONLbonuses.

Chief cook and bottle washer

And yet, you may still be chief cook and bottle washer many times in the course of a week or a month or a year. So wash those bottles.

But remember the key lesson here—even if the daily tasks of your nonprofit have taken thirty hours of your time this week, they are not the *core* of your job. If it helps, think of them as research. Learn the tasks so that you can eventually just fill in when needed or so you can better understand the work that is being done. Approach these tasks with your leader mindset. An employee may not see an opportunity to change a task for the better, but a leader might, because a leader's job is to work *on* the nonprofit.

There's something else to note here as well. If you are taking the time needed to get the decisions right, then your day-to-day work will inevitably become more focused. A little bit of long-term thinking will help make sure that you don't get overwhelmed by whatever is on fire today. Practice this mindset and you'll find that you start encountering fewer and fewer fires that require your immediate attention. And eventually you'll find that the decisions you've been making are opening up new resources (either in terms of time or money) that allow for real growth to happen.

So let's go back to the question we started with.

What does an Executive Director actually do?

She does the work that needs to get done today, but she also keeps a mental distance from it in order to accomplish the real work—leading the organization.

But who exactly are you leading? The community? Volunteers? Staff? The board you ostensibly work for?

What if I told you it was *everyone*?

Herding cats

I often say that a lot of the work of leading a nonprofit is just keeping everyone pointed in the same direction. You can call this herding cats, or a variety of other things. But I would also give you another word for it: politics.

I have served for more than ten years in local elected office. When I ran for office in 2011 and 2017, I campaigned, I made speeches, I listened to constituents. That work made me, by any definition, a politician. And yet, in my experience, the role of Executive Director of a small nonprofit was *more* political than my role as an actual politician.

Take Linda's goal of finding a new way to manage school tours at the pioneer cabin. She's likely going to have a mix of reactions to that plan from a mix of different people. To make it a reality, she'll need to show the teachers that the quality of the tours won't drop. The board might be worried about liability. Her current staff might be worried the job will land in their laps. And, because of the state contract, she might even need someone from the state to sign off. Each group will require a different kind of assurance.

Understanding their concerns and then navigating these waters is the very definition of politics. Which gets us to the next key part of leading for an Executive Director: listening and persuasion.

Listening and persuasion

It's easy to think of the role of Executive Director as, well, *directing* things. Executively so! And this can happen sometimes, of course. You tell an employee, "This is the new strategy we're going to pursue," and it happens.

But most of the time, you will find you are best able to achieve success with lots of listening and lots of persuasion. Small nonprofits often find partners and join coalitions to bring about change in a way they can't affect themselves. These outside groups can't be "directed." Making change in them requires a lot of listening and persuasion.

Even your own staff will benefit from this approach. Remember that everyone at a small nonprofit is there because they *want* to be there. They aren't in it for the money. They aren't in it for the cushy benefits. They want to help. Run roughshod over them all the time and you will soon find that people get tired of it. Tell them it's "my way or the highway" and these folks will eventually choose the highway.

The key point is that you shouldn't fight this part of your job. Listening and persuasion is time-consuming. When it's relational, this means scheduling coffee meetings or phone calls with board members. Or it might mean more one-on-one meetings with staff than you think should be necessary. When listening and persuasion are more formal, it can be just as time-consuming. It means writing good reports for the people or organizations who need them. It means taking an extra hour to rehearse a presentation to the board.

Put in the time.

Broadcasting

There's another kind of listening and persuading that is a big enough deal that it deserves its own heading—talking to donors, members, Facebook followers, and the general public. Nonprofit leaders often make the mistake of assuming that everyone is paying attention to them...until an event tanks due to lack of attendance or an annual appeal fails to make back the cost of postage. Then suddenly there's a flurry of marketing (that more often than not eventually dries up when things seem "fine" again).

As Executive Director, you should make sure you are communicating externally. A monthly email newsletter is a fine start, especially if you have a system in place for getting new people onto it (a sign-up sheet at events, a calendar reminder to add new donors, etc.). But the ED is also the best person to speak at a local Kiwanis club, to attend another nonprofit's luncheon and shake a lot of hands, to be a guest on a local podcast, or perhaps even to start her *own* podcast.

This kind of work can feel overwhelming because there's always more marketing to be done. There are literally an infinite number of options. The best way to manage this is to pick a handful of repeatable tasks you can build systems around and start there. Then accept the special opportunities that you can't really plan for (like speaking to local groups) and call it good.

Tell stories about your success. Invite people to learn more. You know this work better than anyone. Please share it!

Fundraising

Fundraising is another core duty of the Executive Director, yet it's often the role that EDs want to jettison or put off as long as possible.

Many small nonprofit leaders come to an organization for a love of the mission (like Linda) and don't have any background in fundraising (like Linda). It sounds scary and they either ignore it or cast about on ineffective ideas like restaurant takeovers ("Eat at Joe's Pizza tonight and five percent of the proceeds will go to the Smallville Historical Society!") or ideas that are effective only at large nonprofits ("Let's throw a massive gala auction for a thousand people!").

Now, EDs are not *solely* responsible for fundraising. Board members share responsibility here too. But an Executive Director who turns over fundraising entirely to the board will often find that not much happens.

I find that paid staff can be more successful than board members at getting the actual *tasks* of fundraising completed. While board members can be very effective fundraisers when *relationships* are needed. For example, when I was Executive Director of City Club of Tacoma, I staffed the board's membership committee (we treated membership as a fundraising base). At every membership committee meeting, I brought a list of club members that needed to renew, a list of recently renewed members to thank, plus call scripts and call reports to go with them. The committee members and I spent the last ten to fifteen minutes of the meeting calling members and asking if they would like to renew or thanking them for their renewals.

The board members got through far more calls in that time than I would have on my own. And they actually did the calls! (If you send call lists home with board members, there's a good chance they will never get around to making the calls they promised.) After each call, the board member jotted down what happened: Did they renew and give a credit card number? Did they decline? Did the board member leave a voice mail (using the script I provided)?

This was incredibly effective for our membership renewals. My work was to create the container that allowed the board members to do their relational work.

That's just one example of how boards and EDs can share the fundraising work. There are many more. An ED might write the annual appeal and get everything ready for a board envelope-stuffing party. Or perhaps the ED works with a small committee to plan a breakfast fundraiser where the ED takes care of the logistics, but the board takes responsibility for filling the tables with donors. It's a joint effort, for sure, but the ED is best suited to make things happen.

The Executive Director is also the best person to write a grant request. No one knows the organization as well as the ED and no one else (unless you have a full-time grant writer or director of development, which is rare at a small nonprofit) can spend a day writing an application. Grant writing is time-consuming. I often worked on a grant for a few hours here and there before the deadline, but when the actual deadline day came, I blocked out my whole day for it. If you've never written a grant, they are far more time-consuming than you might think, so plan ahead.

Finally, Executive Directors should also expect that they will be the one to ask for any "major gifts." What's a major gift? The answer differs at every nonprofit. It might be $500 or it might be $50,000. It's a gift that is fiscally meaningful to your nonprofit, at an amount that only your very top donors can afford to give. That's a major gift. And at a small nonprofit, there is no one else better suited to ask for that gift than the Executive Director.

I have an entire book about this topic—*The Little Book of Gold: Fundraising for Small (and Very Small) Nonprofits*—if you would like to learn more about how to create a professional fundraising system at your nonprofit that will really help you build something sustainable.

All of that is to say—fundraising is a key part of your work.

Supporting the board

An Executive Director should "staff" the board. I've given some examples in the fundraising section above, but it's much more than that. The ED should look for ways to take *tasks* off the board's plate to make it easier for them to make decisions. For example, a board might want to host a retreat to improve their skills and work on a strategic plan. The Executive Director should jump at the opportunity to find them a location for the retreat and research possible retreat facilitators for the board.

Or let's say the Smallville Historical Society has a membership committee, and the committee spends a lot of time discussing whether or not to change the membership pricing structure. Linda should absolutely jump in and offer to run the numbers to estimate how a pricing model would affect revenue and membership levels.

If a board member offers to do this, it's likely it won't happen. Or—perhaps worse—it's done poorly. What happens if a board member runs the numbers and concludes that the new membership model would be amazing, but Linda spots a bunch of problems with it? It puts her in a tough spot. Now she's correcting "one of her bosses." It makes a lot more sense for the person with the most information (the ED) to take on this kind of work. Then, the committee and eventually the board have the best information to decide whether or not to make the change. This process also allows the ED to put her thumb on the scale, so to speak. Everything goes through the board, but she makes sure she's pushing it in the direction she knows it needs to go.

Here's another important way an ED can staff the board—gentle nudges. For example, the ED might email the chair of a committee and write something like: "I know we canceled our December membership committee meeting but maybe we should get January's meeting on the calendar so we don't miss two months in a row. I have some things I'd love the committee's feedback on. Would you like me to send some dates to the committee members to figure out the best time to meet?"

This is the kind of email that keeps the train on the tracks. Without emails like this, it's just too easy for volunteer board and committee members to fall out of important habits like regular meetings. Gentle nudges like this are well worth doing. And if they say there isn't work to be done, then ask for their help! Present a problem to the committee and see what they think. Keeping a regular meeting on the books is worth the hassle.

There's a whole section later in the book about working with your board that dives deep into this.

Reputation management

When Warren Buffett took over a troubled investment banking firm, he told his employees, "Lose money for the firm, and I will be understanding. Lose a shred of reputation for the firm, and I will be ruthless." EDs of small nonprofits in particular should be sensitive to reputation and ethics. Why? Because as a small nonprofit, there's not much else you have going for you! A big nonprofit caught in a major scandal has time and money to rebrand, market, or otherwise recover. A small nonprofit often doesn't. So pay attention to this. Are you true to your word? Do you apologize for mistakes and oversights in a clear way and then seek to make changes so they don't happen again? Do you spend restricted grants and donations in the way the donor has stipulated?

These things matter. If you play fast and loose with the rules, people will eventually start to notice. Make the decision to do the right thing, even if it costs you some money or time. It pays off in the long run.

Self-improvement

An Executive Director should look for opportunities to improve. Experience is a great teacher, certainly. But you can learn just as much from others' experiences as from your own. Reading this book is a good start!

Try this system—set a quarterly reminder to find a class, workshop, or webinar to attend. It's worth the time to take a couple hours or a half day here and there to brush up your skills. If you can allocate even a couple to a few hundred dollars in the budget for this, it's enough to find high-quality programs in your area or online.

I also recommend finding a peer group of Executive Directors in your area that meet for a drink regularly and share stories, ideas, and advice. I've seen this work well, especially when the group of EDs come from similar-sized nonprofits with low competition and overlap of donors among them. Regular meetups can build a network of trust and openness that can really help. If this doesn't exist, consider being the one to put it together! Invite three or four EDs to join you for a bottle of wine at happy hour (or for an early breakfast if that's your preference) and see what happens!

Aim for growth

You should be growing as an organization, even if it's just a little bit every year. It's simply not enough to tread water.

But how to grow?

Small nonprofit growth usually happens in fits and starts, if at all. Consider a nonprofit that is experiencing an amazing surge in its vitality. Maybe it's driven by a particularly talented staff member or the largesse of a particular donor. But it thrives for a while. And then the nonprofit just sort of...withers. Maybe the star staff member moves on to a better-paying job, or the donor moves on to a new passion. But the growth is gone. Maybe new leadership can get it moving again or maybe not.

Whatever the specifics, the reason a small nonprofit doesn't grow usually boils down to this: *the nonprofit doesn't bring its reasons for success forward into the future.*

It might be doing well right now, yes. But no one is looking over the horizon. So whether it's a successful mission-driven program, a surprisingly effective marketing campaign, or a fundraising event, the ED of a small nonprofit should constantly be asking, "What do I need in order to repeat this again next year?" It's hard for a leader to make the time to do this. It's not always in our nature. But it's the only way a small nonprofit will eventually grow.

To help clarify *how* to go about making this happen, I have created what I call "The Four Ds" that will enable growth at a small nonprofit:

Documentation.

As much as possible, an ED should encourage staff to document their jobs and relationships. How does a particular program work? A program manager could write out a one-page overview and create a checklist for implementation on any given day. If that staff member eventually takes another job elsewhere, you've captured an important part of her work.

Similarly, you might consider leading staff in the development of an annual plan for the organization and each staff member's work. Take a half day and lay out the year with your staff. When are board meetings? When are big important events on your calendar? What needs to happen and when? Capture it and refer to it regularly. These should be living documents too. Set a reminder every three or four months to ask your employees to update their documents.

This idea of documentation applies to your own work as well. What's the timeline for planning the annual fundraiser? If you've just completed it, now is the perfect time to reflect back and lay it out for your future self. (And then set a reminder for when you need to start planning!)

All of this pays off when you have to make a new hire or when you are ready for the next "cycle" (the next fundraising event, the next calendar year, whatever it is). You have something in place. There's a *roadmap*, where before there was none. Without this, a nonprofit that gets a star employee, for example, won't be able to capture her work and help the employees who come after her to implement it. Or the nonprofit will constantly fall behind on the regular cycles—always behind on planning and preparation, because no one had a document in advance that tells them how and when to start.

Database.

Databases are, of course, a form of documentation. But they are so important that they deserve to be called out again specifically. The two most important kinds of databases are donor databases and customer/client databases.

Here's the truth about donors: If you get a $1,000 donation from someone, that's really great! But if you don't know how to approach that donor again next year, then you've squandered a big opportunity. You need to know who gave you the money, how much, and when. (And ideally any specifics about *why* the donor cared enough about you to make this gift.) All too often, nonprofits try to reinvent the wheel with fundraising. But the most successful fundraising usually comes from asking an ever-growing pool of donors for money year after year. It sounds so simple (and also so scary?) when I say it that way. But you can't do it if you don't have a donor database.

Client or customer databases have a different kind of importance from donor databases. Here's a simple example: if your nonprofit offers regular mental health services, and you find an opportunity to create an amazing group retreat experience, how easily could you email all of your current clients and invite them to register? Or consider the performing arts organization that puts on an amazing concert with a musician fresh from Carnegie Hall. When she returns three years later for a special concert, how easily could you email everyone who went to the first show and give them an early chance at tickets? You simply *must* know who you serve, how they interact with you, and how to reach them.

Even social services nonprofits that work with people experiencing homelessness (who may not have a physical address or a phone) may find benefits of even limited data collection.

Again, remember this is all about being able to repeat success in the future. A nonprofit sitting around and wondering how to reach its donors or clients will always be stuck reinventing the wheel.

Development.

The staff at a small nonprofit will change regularly, but some will stick around for long enough that they can really grow into a position. Working with your staff to build their skills—to develop as an individual and as a team—will pay off. Spend time and money on professional development for everyone on your team. Help them grow.

But this doesn't just mean webinars and classes. It also means, for example, sitting together as a team after a major event and talking about what worked and what could be improved. (And then capturing that conversation to implement the recommendations a year later.) It means finding ways to meet with other similar nonprofits and then sharing expertise, ideas, and resources between your two staffs.

Developing yourself and your staff doesn't have to cost a lot. But finding time to help them do their jobs better (and then capturing what they learn!) will help the nonprofit over time.

Determination.

Finally, a small nonprofit looking to grow does need the determination of you, the ED, to fight for growth. And it will take determination. First, you will need the determination to push others to accept and agree to growth, and then you will need the determination to actually make it happen.

Growth can mean change and change can be scary, which is why you need to push others toward it (staff and board members both may have reasons to be resistant). And you will need to have determination to actually make it happen because—at a small nonprofit—you're the one who is going to write the big grant application. You're the one who is going to invest the time and the heart into making a program truly transformational in a community.

The key to know is this: your determination alone is not

enough to grow a nonprofit. Please don't kill yourself with hundred-hour workweeks and a Herculean effort that saps your soul and burns you out. Your energy and your passion and your determination (and, yes, a few long days here and there) will fuel the nonprofit, so long as you're directing it appropriately. You need the rest—documentation, databases, and development —to make growth stick.

If you are uncertain how to go about leading change at your nonprofit, I've created a special bonus chapter on leading change. As with the other bonus content for this book, it's downloadable at http://bit.ly/LBONLbonuses.

And that's the job

Your job, should you choose to accept it, is to work on the nonprofit (not in it), lead through effective decision-making, manage the operations, persuade and listen to stakeholders, broadcast the mission, fundraise, support the board, manage the reputation, adhere to ethical standards, improve your own skills, and lead growth.

I'm going to guess that much of this is not on your official job description.

But the trick is, you do have to do the things in the job description as well. You have to implement the program. You have to manage the physical space of the nonprofit and whatever else your job description says. (And, just to make sure it's clear again, you can delegate these tasks too. You don't need the board's permission to delegate so long as the tasks get done.)

Rather than me *adding* to your task list, then, think of this chapter as holding up a series of lenses or filters through which to view your day-to-day routine. What parts of the job are you already doing that could be slightly amended—or even just *seen* differently—that could help you start changing how you lead the nonprofit?

One note on all this: transitions take time. If in the spring, Linda decides she needs to get out of leading school tours, that's probably not a change that will be ready until the next school year. Change takes time, especially if you want it to stick.

If you can systematize or delegate some small tasks, that might open up a few hours each week for more marketing or more board support—whatever you think is most needed. Or if you can make a key decision that opens up a new opportunity, you can use the revenues or space created by that to shuffle things in a way that better suits where you're trying to take the organization (and your own time).

But if you announce to the board that you read a book by this Erik Hanberg guy, and he says your job should actually be A, B, and C, and therefore you're not doing X, Y, and Z anymore, well...that's not going to work, let's just put it that way. So think of this early chapter as a way to shape your work over time.

I want to give a few last pointers on the topic of "what is an ED's job" and this idea that change can take time is a good place to start.

Success is measured in years

I've found that this is true of both nonprofits and government. Yesterday looks a lot like today and there's no reason to think that tomorrow will look much different. Change takes time and success is often measured in years.

By this time next year, though, you have the power to take the organization to a whole new place. Maybe not as much as you wish you could, but you can make a noticeable and impactful change.

Yes, sometimes change happens all at once in a way that you can't predict (like the COVID-19 crisis). In those scenarios, the more you can develop a vision for where you want to take the nonprofit, the more likely you will be to emerge from sudden change on a better path than the one you were on.

The nonprofit will be shaped by you

Here's something to know about the Executive Director role: left unchecked, the nonprofit will slowly start to mold itself in your image. You know how two people who have been married for fifty years often look more and more alike as they age? Well, something similar is happening here. The nonprofit will start to look like you. Because everyone is taking their cues from you.

Your strengths will become the organization's strengths. Your weaknesses will become the organization's weaknesses. Let's take a nonprofit ED who excels at organization but has poor interpersonal skills. Over time, the nonprofit will tend to mirror her. This can happen in a variety of ways, but it's easiest to see in the employees. Very likely, people she hires will also be good at organization and will lack strong interpersonal skills. Why? Because she likely won't want to hire people who are highly social but disorganized. Maybe she will call it a bad "culture" fit, but she will be drawn to candidates who are organized the same way she is. The other way that this can happen is that the highly social but disorganized people won't want to work with her because she won't seem like much fun to them. They'll self-select out.

Over time, she'll create a nonprofit with great organization (a benefit if she's administering state grants or other complicated processes) but not very good at raising money from major donors (because everyone at the nonprofit would rather die than pick up the phone and call someone).

This can be true of staff, volunteers, and board members alike. The tone is set by the ED. A cautious and fiscally restrained ED will create a cautious and fiscally restrained organization. An ED quick to say yes to new ideas will create a nonprofit that does the same. And the longer the ED is in place, the more their personality will shape the organization.

If you're perfect, you'll create a perfect nonprofit, so why worry, right?

But, alas, something tells me you're not perfect.

The solution: know thyself.

The more self-awareness you have about your own blind spots and shortcomings, the better you will be at filling those in with new hires instead of hiring people with the same set of strengths and weaknesses you have. Really do an honest assessment. What are you great at? Where could you use help? Look for people who excel in the areas you don't.

Asking for forgiveness not permission

When it came to making a decision like restructuring how to manage school tours, the first thing Linda did was call her board chair.

In general, I believe you should never surprise your board chair at a board meeting. Anything you are prepared to share, the board chair should already know. Your life will be a lot smoother if you stick to that principle.

And yet...when it comes to operations, don't forget who is in charge. You, the Executive Director. You run the show. For many small- and even medium-sized changes, you don't need a special call to your board chair or anything like that. Write a one-page report to the board each month about things you've done and highlight actions you've taken.

You *do* need to calibrate which things are big enough to

warrant getting the board's buy-in. And sometimes you might get it wrong. But for most things, put them in your report as action steps you've already taken.

What's next?

This should be a good start for understanding your role. Next, we need to deeply investigate three areas to really help you get a handle on your nonprofit:

- *Mission*—the core services and programs you provide
- *People*—the staff and volunteers who do the work
- *Money*—the actual dollars and cents that pay for it all

Each will get a separate chapter. While these are presented distinctly, though, the topics are—of course—tightly interconnected. If you want to improve the quality of your program, you will need more money for more employees (or higher quality employees). Each chapter can be a different lens you can use to approach a single project.

TWO
THE MISSION

NONPROFITS EXIST FOR A PURPOSE—THE mission. It's a guiding light for all you do.

But, in the US at least, it's actually more than that. It's the reason your community and your country have given your nonprofit special tax benefits. The Internal Revenue Service actually cares about your mission. If a nonprofit's mission is to "save the whales" but all they are really doing is selling T-shirts that have pictures of whales on them, then they aren't fulfilling the mission of that nonprofit (they are committing tax fraud, technically).

The mission of your nonprofit is not something that you should idly change. It's the organizing principle of everything you do! Certainly, a nonprofit might consider "wordsmithing" its mission every few years, but other than that, it's rare that it should actually *change*. Not without a really good reason.

Learn your mission

An Executive Director needs to know her nonprofit's mission statement by heart. It might sound weird that I think you should memorize a sentence, but it's a very important sentence! Take a few minutes and memorize it. Post it by your desk in a place where you can see it regularly. If, during a committee meeting, a board member asks what the mission is, you should not be the one trying to pull it up on the "About" page of your website!

Learn it.

Now, *live it*

You should be the most strident keeper of the mission. That means not only do you need to have it memorized, you need to internalize it in a very deep way. What does your mission *really* mean? Here's a question to get you started: How should a person's life change if they encounter your nonprofit?

This might initially seem easy to identify if you run a homeless shelter, let's say. A person who comes in gets a place to sleep for the night. That's vitally important. But I bet if you look at your mission statement, it dreams that your organization will do more than just provide a bed for the night. You probably *are* doing more than just providing a bed for the night. Done right, you are comforting someone in a time of crisis. You are providing human connection. You are identifying resources that might support their journey out of homelessness. Dig deeper and really think about the change you are trying to enact in the world.

Look for stories

You don't have to just imagine how someone's life should change, though. Hopefully you've already touched people's lives enough to make a positive impact. But a nonprofit ED can often miss these stories because it is the front-line staff or volunteers who are closest to the work. The ticket taker sees the child's eyes light up at coming to the theater. The volunteer at the food bank hears the story of the family who desperately needed this meal. The volunteer mentor sees the at-risk teenager choose a new path. The ED behind a desk doesn't always get to see these moments.

So ask for stories regularly. Seek them out in staff meetings, in one-on-ones, and when you get to mix with the people you serve. Did something really wonderful happen at the front desk? Or something adorable on a school tour? Did a formerly homeless client call and say that thanks to your nonprofit she now has a home?

Ask for these stories and then—a very important step—write them down! Many nonprofits fall down on this step. The stories are inspiring for the staff but no one captures them for later use. You should be the story keeper. Have a dedicated notebook, or just a Word document on your computer where you can write down the stories you hear. These stories will help you stay connected, but they will also be fodder for your board and donors, who also want to be connected to your mission! They can be used in fundraising appeals, marketing, and more. What moves and inspires you is likely to move and inspire them too. And if one story doesn't resonate, well, you have a whole list of stories.

As you collect these stories over time, look for commonalities. How do other people talk about your organization? What precisely did you do to help someone? You might find good ways to frame your own work.

But there's another task you can do here as well: reflect on why you don't hear the stories more often. If you serve a thousand people a year, but you only get a heartwarming story from a handful of them, what's the reason? Sometimes this could be because a nonprofit serves a population that is incredibly difficult to reach and therefore it's hard to hear how they are doing. Sometimes it's because the systemic problems you are fighting against are so overwhelming that not everyone will have a heartwarming story. But sometimes it's because the nonprofit is not rising to the occasion.

Consider setting a personal goal. If this year you heard five or ten success stories from your clients, what would it take to double that next year? What lessons can you learn from the success stories you've already heard to try to transform the lives of even more of the people you serve?

Don't discount data

There's an old saying that the plural of anecdotes is not data. I just spent a while talking about the virtues of stories. Stories are an essential part of your work. But they aren't everything. Stories plus data are even more powerful for managing your nonprofit's mission and program. Let's check in on Linda, who is about to get a sense of what it's like to begin collecting data.

Linda's school tours

As Linda was preparing to hand off the school tours to someone else (though she wasn't sure who) she quickly realized that she didn't really have anything to actually hand off. There was no script for the school tours. There was no stated learning objective. She just led a group of students through the cabin and the grounds and talked about different things.

It was a surprising revelation to her. In trying to formalize the tours to get them ready to be delegated, she realized that the tours weren't nearly as good as they should be. When she had taken the job a year before, she had briefly overlapped with the previous Executive Director and had shadowed him as he led the tour. She was still basically following the same format. She hadn't really liked doing the tours and she hadn't actually tried to improve them much.

But now she had new eyes on them and realized that a lot more could be done.

She had two school tours scheduled in the week ahead. She decided to lead the tours basically as she had been doing. The difference: she was going to capture data about them. But what kind of data would be useful?

She did some brainstorming and decided that, for now, she'd track as much data as seemed reasonable, and then later she'd review it and keep only the important information.

She created a form to fill out after each tour. She wanted to capture the date, how many kids were on the tour, their grade, their school, their teacher, the teacher's contact information, and whether that teacher had brought them for a tour before. So those were the basics, and much of this information she'd already had to report to the state anyway as part of the contract.

Then she added some places to track her own sense of how the school tour went.

What did the kids respond to really well? When did they seem bored? It was just a place for notes, something her "future self" could look over and use to spot trends. Then, she had a place to score the tour from one to five. It was entirely subjective, of course, but if she was consistent with it, it would be meaningful information. She kept the form to a single page, because anything longer seemed like it would be onerous.

As she looked at it, she also thought about how this form would be used in a few months if a staff member submitted it after leading a tour. That prompted her to add a place to write who led the tour. For now, it would be her own name. Was this enough to give her useful information about how the tours were going, even if she wasn't doing them every day?

That changed her thinking. And she realized that while it was a good start, it still wasn't enough. If she were committed to collecting data, then she needed outside feedback.

So she started on the next form.

This form would go to the teachers. She put a place for their basic information and then asked questions about how the tour fit with their class curriculum, whether there were any additional learning objectives they thought could be incorporated, and then asked for their own evaluation of the program from one to five. Comparing their score to hers could be interesting. Or it might not be! She would gather both for a while and see which number was more useful to her.

Now she looked at everything she'd put together, and she realized that it *still* didn't capture as much as she wanted. What she was really interested in understanding was what the kids learned and what they thought of the tour. But she didn't think she could get them to fill out a form.

She did some research and found that there were ways to ask questions before a tour that would give her a baseline understanding of their knowledge level and then she could ask questions at the end that would cement what they had learned. She was deep in the weeds of educational practices—much more than she'd ever been before—but it was actually motivating her. Even if she couldn't hand off the tours for some time, she thought this was going to make her feel better about leading them until then.

Evaluating programs with data

Gathering data is an important part of evaluating your nonprofit's program. The right data will depend on your services. It's worth taking time to see what the best practices are for your field. Whatever field you're in, there are almost certainly recommendations on the kind of data you should collect and review. The key is to make data collection a system and then to do something useful with it.

At the Grand Cinema, I created an Excel spreadsheet that every house manager filled out at the end of the night. It covered ticket sales, concession sales, and total revenue for the day. The next day when I came into work, I took that sheet and plugged a few of those numbers into a master spreadsheet that I created. My master spreadsheet had the data for every single day the Grand had been in existence. Building that huge spreadsheet took *days*, because my predecessor hadn't tracked it, so I went back and entered data on seven years' worth of daily attendance. Keeping it updated, though, took less than a minute a day. That spreadsheet was hugely helpful. I could average years' worth of seasonality in our business and forecast how we might do for a given season. I could take it and model the effect of ticket prices, for example, and much more. Those numbers also featured regularly in my monthly report to the board.

Tracking attendance and revenue is relatively easy. The numbers are measuring real things that anyone can objectively agree on.

The other kind of data uses soft numbers, and it's much harder to track and carries with it a lot of caveats. But it can still be revealing. Linda eventually tracked the teachers' evaluation of the school tours, how the students on the field trip answered her questions at the end of the tour (to evaluate their comprehension), and her own estimation of how the tour went. The key to making this exercise worthwhile is simplicity and consistency. And keep your reporting forms the same for as long as you can. The ability to compare numbers between months or years only works if you're collecting the numbers in the same way!

You can collect this kind of data in the moment, the way Linda was. Some arts organizations send surveys to patrons the day after a show, as another example. If it's a lot of work to collect this kind of data in the moment, though, the other option is to plan for regular collection. Even a quarterly day of data gathering is better than none at all. Members, patrons, customers, and other stakeholders can be surveyed via an online form. Figure out what data you want, how to collect it regularly, and take the time every so often to evaluate it.

Here are a couple ways you can use this data to improve your programs:

Look for discrepancies.

If Linda gave a tour a good score but the teacher didn't, that might cause her to reach out with additional questions. If she hadn't collected the data, she might have thought the tour had gone really well, not knowing the teacher was dissatisfied.

Watch for trends in the data.

If teacher ratings start consistently dropping, that's meaningful information for Linda to research. So one terrible review from a teacher isn't necessarily a systemic problem (though, again, it's well worth Linda looking into!) but a string of mediocre reviews suggests she needs to make some changes.

Use data to boost revenue.

This is jumping ahead to the money section, but you can use program data to improve your overall revenue as well. There are several ways, but I'll give you just one example. At the Grand Cinema, I had a significant amount of data to sort through from a comprehensive member survey. One piece of data in there was interesting—members reported that they came to the Grand twelve times a year. Seeing a movie once a month seemed high to me. I turned to my spreadsheet of ticket attendance and did a simple bit of math. I divided the total number of member tickets sold by the total number of members. And I discovered that the *average* member came to the Grand only four times a year.

These two numbers were incredibly useful when viewed together. When we changed our membership pricing, we priced it to be a really good deal if you came twelve times a year, as our members *thought* they did, but for those who used the member discount closer to four times a year, it was really helpful to our bottom line. This was a great place to price our membership, and it was only revealed by looking at the data.

Show that you are paying attention.

There's another benefit of tracking data. Collecting data on your programs shows your staff, volunteers, and board that you are paying attention. It's a good way to start seeing everyone else start making improvements in how they go about enacting your mission too. "That which is measured gets improved," as the old saying goes. When people know you're tracking something, it will improve.

Evaluating your programs in addition to data

I love poring over data and delving into spreadsheets. The trends (and the exceptions to the trends) that can be revealed have helped me make a lot of important decisions. But data isn't everything. It's a tool in the tool belt, but it shouldn't guide all that you do.

This is especially true the more your data measures intangible things. The more you try to capture the ephemeral, the more it's going to slip away from you. You need other ways to think about your program.

Is the program aligned with your mission?

The first is to simply hold it up to your nonprofit's mission. You've memorized it, so let's put it to work! Is your program aligned with your mission? Is it rising to meet those lofty goals or falling short? Sometimes programs can start to exceed their original purpose, either in pursuit of new funds or just through a slow but steady bloating process. This is called "mission creep." Look for parts of your program that may have grown into something that doesn't truly fit with what you do and then figure out how to refocus them. A tight program will be much stronger.

And, again, if your mission has big aspirational words in it, look for ways to try to live up to those goals in the programs you already have. Linda might try to build in a moment at the beginning or end of the school tour with a dash of wonder: "Imagine that this is the only building for miles...you're all on your own in a cabin you built with your own hands. You're hungry. You're lonely. And then what should appear on the horizon...but a covered wagon! Carrying food and bringing a new family. How would that feel?" Yes, it's melodramatic. But sometimes a little schmaltz or a little melodrama goes a long way.

Would the program look different with someone else in charge?

The next way to evaluate a program is to see how it looks with different people leading it. You can use people's vacation and sick time to see what a program looks like when someone else is in charge. This is *not* about getting rid of the regular program supervisor. But as you watch someone else in the role for a bit, you might notice a new spark you hadn't seen before. Perhaps it will give you an idea for what the regular program lead could be doing. Seeing what new ideas look like in practice can be very useful.

(There are other good reasons to cross-train a team at a small nonprofit. Turnover can unfortunately be high at small nonprofits and programs often rely on a single person to implement them. Should that person leave suddenly, it can cause turmoil and the program can suffer. Cross-training can help fill in the gaps while you hire.)

How would this program look in a different location?

Location, location, location. It's true in real estate and it's true for nonprofits—the specific location you choose for a program can make a real difference to the quality of the program and experience of the participants.

Imagine for a moment that whatever location you use for your program was no longer available. (This may not take a lot of imagining if you have already experienced this disruption during the COVID-19 pandemic.) If you couldn't put on your program where you normally do, where would you go? If the pioneer cabin were unavailable due to structural repairs, let's say, Linda might consider programming in a nearby park or bringing historical artifacts to the schools themselves. This could even become a separate program.

On the flip side, a nonprofit that often works out in the community may find economies of scale and other social benefits by centralizing services in a single location.

Rethinking some core assumptions of your work will help you adapt if you are ever forced into a corner or find better ways to serve your community.

Is the program going to be a priority in the future?

And finally, you can think about your program with an eye toward the future. Is this sustainable over the long term? Is this the kind of thing you want the nonprofit to be doing in five years?

Sometimes it's clear that a program, due to demographics or some other issue, will either eventually die or take a massive effort to save. Imagine a nonprofit that provides social services to active adults and seniors, and for years they've hosted a chess tournament that's a big revenue maker because people come from all over the state to compete. But in the last five years or so, the number of people who enter the tournament has gotten smaller and smaller and the people who remain are older and older. At some point that nonprofit ED will have to ask whether it's going to be sustainable to keep hosting it.

One option she could choose is to let it slowly shrink and chalk it up to lack of interest by the new generation while looking for some other kind of program to ramp up to meet the needs and interests of her community. Or, she could start hosting chess lessons, bring in chess grandmasters, and generally try to get more people inspired about chess. There's not necessarily a right answer. Although I would ask her this question: How important is chess to the actual mission of the organization? If the same purpose could be accomplished with a different activity, would the mission be fulfilled?

Sometimes things like that can be given a second life, and sometimes larger societal or demographic forces mean that a program may just have to fade away through no one's fault. Whether to let it die slowly or to invest the resources to try to revive it is ultimately up to you. It's a question of how closely a program like this is tied to your mission and whether you think you can marshal the efforts needed to save something.

Who are you serving?

This last example of a nonprofit thinking about the demographics of who attends their chess tournament leads us to another important question: Who exactly are you serving with your mission? Or perhaps, more accurately, who are you *not* serving? There are two ways that nonprofits end up focusing on a certain demographic to serve: *intentionally* and *unintentionally*.

A nonprofit can intentionally focus their services in a variety of ways and those ways are likely called out specifically in your mission. You might have a focus on:

- age (such as youth services or senior services)
- gender or orientation (such as LGBT resources or women's groups)
- race, religion, ethnicity, or another cultural group (such as the NAACP, a church, or the Sons of Norway)

- geography (a neighborhood business district, a statewide professional association)
- and, finally, a nonprofit may intentionally focus on a certain slice of the population based on their experience more than their demographics (such as a homeless shelter or the Red Cross)

Expanding or contracting your intentional area of focus is a big deal. It likely takes an explicit change of your mission, and you will need buy-in from your board and maybe even the wider community to do it. But, as the ED, it's definitely worth thinking about! What would your nonprofit look like if you served not only your city, but a neighboring one as well? Who could you serve if your nonprofit expanded its educational focus from elementary school to early learning (birth to age five) as well? What if a homeless shelter expanded programs to serve people once they get housed so that they don't fall back into a cycle of poverty?

Or, alternatively, what if you narrowed focus from the entire school district to just one middle school? Could you make an incredibly deep impact on the lives of those kids? Or what if instead of serving youth from birth until high school, you focused on early learning and dramatically improving preschool standards? Going narrow may have just as many benefits as going wide can.

These are great lenses with which to look at your nonprofit, and it's worth it as an Executive Director to think about whether any of these opportunities could create something exciting for your organization and the people you serve. There can be strength in the added revenue streams or the intentional focus these kinds of decisions can bring about. You may find you can serve your community even better.

But possibly even more important than that is this question:

When you think about the people you serve, who are you *unintentionally* leaving out?

Many, *many* nonprofits unintentionally leave out people based on their gender (such as a male-dominated professional group), age (such as an arts organization mostly enjoyed by retired people), or race (such as any one of a vast number of nonprofits that end up serving white clientele despite being in a diverse community).

I'll give you a simple example of this. When I was at the Grand Cinema, we had a membership base that was predominantly white and retired. (This is very common for many arts organizations.) But I vividly recall a weekend where we had two Spanish-language films playing at the same time. So out of three theaters, two screens were playing Spanish-language movies, and we suddenly had a lot of native Spanish speakers buying tickets. The audience looked visibly different from a "normal" weekend at the Grand.

This was a clear case where changing a program (from English-language to Spanish-language) served a new audience. But you should look at this example as the exception rather than the rule. Many nonprofits try to expand their appeal to new demographics and fail. Why? Because they view it as a problem of *marketing*, not as a problem of who they are. A well-meaning Executive Director might ask: "How can we go out and get more women into our group?" or "How can we reach more young people?" or "How can we bring in more people of color?" Those are good questions to ask, but here's what I've learned— these issues are usually not a problem with marketing. It's usually a much bigger issue and it will take real change to appeal to a new audience.

Again, I'll give you an example from my own background.

At City Club of Tacoma, our organization was founded by people in the 1980s who were "mid-to-late career." As they aged, they never replaced themselves, so to speak. Generationally speaking, these were either the silent generation or maybe some of the oldest boomers. Younger boomers (the next generation who would have joined the club) culturally weren't really "joiners," though. Gen X wasn't particularly interested either. And while millennials actually had some interest, it wasn't enough to really change the makeup of the overall club. So the club had a lot of retired folks and a few young folks. I worked hard to try to appeal to the same "mid-to-late career" folks who founded the club (just twenty-five years later). It wasn't as easy as just marketing to them, though. The whole *vibe* of the club was wrong. Our lunch meetings, for example, were held in a musty meeting hall that hadn't been updated in decades. It was also far enough away from downtown Tacoma that working professionals would need to go get their car from a parking garage, drive to the meeting, attend the meeting, drive back to their parking garage, and then walk back to work. It added at least a half hour to the meeting for them, and most of them weren't willing to do it.

So I researched new opportunities for the lunch meetings and found a great room in a downtown museum that was much more centrally located. It was sleek, modern, and within easy walking distance for far more downtown workers.

Personally speaking, it was more of a headache to make this happen because it required me to both find the venue and to manage the new challenges of being there. But the plan worked! Over the next two years, the downtown lunch programs started being attended by younger and younger audiences, while the evening dinner programs kept their same retired audience. By the time I left, the attendees at the City Club lunch programs had an average age that was ten or twenty years younger than when I'd started.

I also started adding special programs that we booked in

bars, coffee shops, art galleries, and other nontraditional locations. This was a great way to host forums and participate in the civic dialogue that could reach an entirely new audience.

What City Club was facing was not a question of marketing. What we had been doing simply wasn't appealing to the demographics we wanted. We needed to change how (and where) we offered our programs to begin to draw in a new audience.

Better marketing or new programs *can* help you reach new audiences. But just as often there's a cultural or systemic issue preventing some people from using your services. To truly reach them, you will have to make real change in what you offer and how you go about it.

Doing this effectively takes a keen amount of listening and working with the community you are trying to draw in (as opposed to just guessing). A nonprofit struggling to attract people of color needs to actually talk to people of color to shape programs!

That said, it's still often not enough. Change may need to happen at all levels—like even adding new board members, staff members, and new programs at (roughly) the same time.

That might sound like I keep setting the bar higher and higher, but there's a reason it can be so difficult. If the non-arts EDs will indulge me for a moment, let's take the example from the world of theater. Theater companies have tried to expand their diversity with supposedly "color-blind" casting. And yet, invariably, the results are plays cast predominantly with white actors. Why? One reason might be unconscious bias on the part of the artistic directors, of course. Another reason is that, systemically, there are far fewer actors of color in the theater. Many people of color have not been cast in leading roles throughout their entire lives—whether in high school, college, or professionally—due to systemic racism and a lack of parts written for people of color. So they drop out, find other work, or make a career with lesser roles.

What that systemic problem means is that for any individual casting decision, a theater's artistic director can always point to a résumé and say, "See, this person has a wealth of experience and fits the role perfectly, while this person has only had a few big parts. I clearly cast the best actor—the fact that I cast the white actor and not the person of color isn't on me. Would it be fair to cast the less-qualified actor?"

Now, she very well may have cast the best actor for the part. But, taken in the aggregate, all of these individual artistic directors are making individual decisions that still lead to the same systemic problem—white actors being cast overwhelmingly over actors of color.

So what is that one artistic director to do in the face of systemic bias? She is in a cycle that won't end without significant change at all levels—more color-blind casting, more plays written with parts explicitly for people of color, and more theater classes offered to young people of color. How can one theater make a dent in the face of that?

To quote Apple's CEO Tim Cook in his public announcement that he was gay, "We pave the sunlit path toward justice together, brick by brick. This is my brick."

So that's my question to you: What is your nonprofit's brick?

I don't know what your brick is, but there's *something* you can do. Every kind of nonprofit is struggling with these questions, and if you set out to find out what others are doing, you will surely find good places to start.

If all of this is overwhelming, I understand. It may be easy for the male-dominated board to give lip service to the idea of bringing on more women—but when you advocate for real change to make the organization more appealing to women, some board members are going to get defensive. That can be challenging and discouraging for the ED who wants to expand the audience and bring in the people who have been unintentionally left out.

As a practical first step, if you want to reach out to a new audience, here's a place to start: find partner organizations to work with that get you closer to where you want to go. Whomever you are trying to reach out to, you will find groups that already serve that group and do it well. How can you work together on a joint program, a forum, or some other kind of pilot project? Let the partner organization lead the way, and see what you can do to support them. This is a pretty good way to start. You'll learn more about where your own blind spots are and discover new ways to live your mission. You will meet people different from yourself and create new relationships. As you gain experience from these partnerships, it will become clearer to you what changes you may need to make in your own organization.

How are you serving your community?

In addition to the population you serve, you can also evaluate at what level you are best suited to help that population. One organization might provide housing to homeless veterans. This is vital, of course, but a nonprofit like this will often run into issues of capacity. They only have so many beds and when the need is too great, they have to turn people away. Another nonprofit might take a different approach. They might focus on advocacy and spend their energies lobbying city and state government for more affordable housing in general. This approach won't directly help the veterans who are experiencing homelessness *tonight* like the other nonprofit is. On the one hand, they might be able to make larger systemic changes over time. On the other hand, they also are less connected to the on-the-ground experience of people suffering right now. Both options are right! Both options are needed. And there are almost certainly several in-between options as well. The question is: Where does your nonprofit fit on this spectrum?

Turning weakness into strength

We often think about someone's greatest strength also being their greatest weakness. This is true for businesses and nonprofit organizations as well. You just need the mentality to see it.

Instead of bemoaning that you're not as big or well-funded as the larger nonprofits in your area, turn your size into your strength. Small nonprofits are nimble and can move quickly when they need to. Sometimes a staff of five can deliver a new program much faster (and sometimes even better) than a staff of twenty. Fewer meetings...fewer roadblocks...fewer people who need to sign off. A good idea can sometimes get off the ground much faster at a small nonprofit.

So in those times when the weaknesses of your organization are frustrating you, look to the ways they also give you strength. Even a weakness that is endemic to small nonprofits, such as high turnover, can be seen as a strength—it's easier to pivot to the needs of the market with a regular infusion of fresh eyes.

At the same time, let's not be too Pollyannaish about this. Having more resources is usually better than having fewer, even if there are creative ways you can leverage having fewer. But if you *do* have fewer, you may as well lean into the strengths you have.

Learn to love pilot projects

As you use the ideas here to improve your program delivery, you might find ideas for new programs to launch, so I will close the chapter with a way to move forward with new plans.

People, in general, don't like to fail. The way that manifests itself at work is that people don't want to disappoint their boss or the customers or the public. So they put off launching programs that might lose money (or might simply lose face). It's a problem if you want to lead the kind of nonprofit that tries new things.

If you set up the right conditions, risking failure can be managed. This is where pilot projects can come in. If you have a good idea but you aren't totally sure if it will actually work, then look for ways to test it with the lowest possible stakes.

There are a few essential features to a good pilot program.

The first is telling your board explicitly *in advance* that you are testing an idea that may not work and have already taken steps to make sure there's no long-term harm. In short: you need to establish the possibility of failure and simultaneously indicate how you are addressing it before you even start.

For example, Linda might go to her board and say, "Later this summer, we will be testing a new idea that shows a lot of potential—a dramatic reenactment of the labor riots from the 1920s. It's a play written by a long-time volunteer at the Historical Society and I think it could be a big opportunity. But it's a new idea for us, and we don't know if our audience will necessarily turn out. To be frank—it might flop. I've already reached out to the Smallville Little Theater and they are going to partner with us on the production and share in the costs. We've gotten a small grant for the sets too, which means that there's very little downside left because that's the majority of our costs, and the rest is split with the theater.

"If it's successful, there's real potential for long-term revenue from it because we can stage it every year or tour it to schools. And if it's not successful, well, it was a worthy effort for a summer production and we leave it at that."

Notice how Linda is also framing the other key ingredient of pilot projects—she is stating quite clearly from the start how the pilot will end. Knowing this internally is important but also make sure that there is no promise of anything longer-term in your marketing. If you want to create an annual conference to address affordable housing issues in your state, but you don't know that it will work, then create and market "a special one-day conference." See how it goes, without the promise of later conferences. If it works, try it again when it feels right. And if after that, it still feels like people want it, great. Make it an annual event. But if it doesn't work, it was a nice attempt and no one knows you "failed."

Consider the alternative: You want to start a special monthly concert series at your local theater. You announce it to big fanfare, but six months later, attendance has cratered, the series is losing money, and you don't know how to get out of it without losing face. Instead, piloting a special set of "three spring concerts" gives you a lot of cover if it doesn't work.

Look for ways to reduce expenses, inch into new programs, and give yourself plenty of "outs" before you commit to anything ongoing.

———

With all those ways to evaluate and improve your program, it's time to move on to the people who run your nonprofit. Because programs aren't anything without people.

THREE

THE PEOPLE

A SMALL NONPROFIT is only as strong as the employees and volunteers who run it. A small group of dedicated, intelligent, and compassionate people working or volunteering at a small nonprofit can do amazing things. And leading that team as the Executive Director is an amazing experience.

But there are always bumps in the road. Leading and managing people is hard!

This chapter is all about working with people—the equal parts difficult, joyful, maddening, and inspiring people who will make up your staff and volunteers.

You need them, and they need you. (Trust me, they need you.)

Linda's staff

Linda had two employees: a part-time bookkeeper and a full-time employee whose title was membership coordinator but who was really a jill-of-all-trades. She had inherited both of them from the previous Executive Director and they were both...fine.

The bookkeeper was sometimes severe or condescending when Linda submitted reimbursement receipts and Linda felt that she was just overall difficult to work with. But the books got done and they seemed free from mistakes, so she didn't know if she should complain too much. And didn't it make sense to have an eagle-eyed bookkeeper? she asked herself.

The membership coordinator was young and enthusiastic about everything at the Historical Society, but she was often late to arrive at work in the morning and made a lot of mistakes in her writing—that in particular caused no end of frustration for Linda, who hated making even the smallest typo. Linda liked her a lot as a person, but she certainly wouldn't have hired her for the job. But when Linda had finally found time to take a week-long vacation with her family, it was the membership coordinator who had held things together in her absence. That surely counted for something?

Linda didn't want to fire her employees—far from it. But she *did* want a lot more out of them. She didn't know where to start.

Why do people work at small nonprofits?

To understand how to work with employees, we need to know why they are at a small nonprofit. And I'm here to tell you, it's not the money!

Small nonprofits' pay is usually pretty poor versus larger nonprofits or for-profit businesses. So why do people work for small nonprofits? Here are the main reasons:

- *Love of the mission.* If you're going to give up higher pay, it's usually because you love the nonprofit's mission. This is the most compelling reason to work at a small nonprofit. You want to make a difference for a particular cause, and here's a place to do it.

- *Flexibility and quality of life.* In general, small nonprofits can often provide more flexibility than other jobs. Do you want to be able to pick up your kids every day at 3:30 after school and work from home after that? A small nonprofit is much more likely to make that work than a for-profit. The exchange (again) is that you aren't earning as much. But it's a nice benefit.

- *Experience building.* At the age of twenty-two, just out of college, I was working in marketing and event planning at a small nonprofit. I was doing work *way* outside of what my résumé said I was qualified to do. But it was significant enough work that at twenty-three, I was hired to be the managing director of a different nonprofit, the Grand Cinema, based in many ways on the reputation I'd made for myself at the first job. This is true for many folks, whether they are young, as I was, or just looking for a career change.

Usually, these factors are most powerful when they work together. Consider a mother in her early thirties who starts working part-time at a small educational nonprofit when her kids become school-age. She has a love of the mission, she wants the flexibility, and she's looking to build her professional experience. A perfect fit.

But fast-forward a couple years when her kids are older. She doesn't need as much flexibility in her schedule, her abilities have grown, and she wants more professional opportunities.

She'll be well-suited to take her experience to a new organization if you can't find ways for her to grow at your nonprofit.

Actually managing employees

I've often seen (and sometimes personally felt) a reluctance among Executive Directors to actually *manage* employees. There can be a tendency to want to "let employees do their jobs." Which may work just fine until something goes wrong. Now you're pulling an employee into your office to grill them and you discover that you don't really know what they've been doing at all.

You should be in regular communication with any employee you directly supervise. For many kinds of employees, the best way to do this is a weekly check-in. Spend a half hour or an hour together and check in on the biggest items the employee is working on. It's also a good time to delegate new tasks and talk over new projects. This is great in situations where you don't naturally work closely with someone, where their work is project based, or where the work changes frequently.

For employees doing more routine work or shift work, find reasons to be present when your employees are working. Check in on them during quiet times, or lend a hand during busy times. Observe how your employees work and "catch them doing something right" regularly and commend them:

"Oh, thank you for dusting the front desk today! It looks so good. What a thoughtful touch."

"I was listening in to how you handled that upset patron. You were clear and polite. Keep it up!"

"This spreadsheet is so clear and useful. It helps me understand the program a lot better. Thank you for taking the initiative on it!"

These moments with staff are also the appropriate places to coach and direct their work. That means direct and clear communication about ways they could do their job better. For the conflict-averse out there, I have to say very clearly that you owe it to your employees and to the nonprofit to do this. If you have certain standards, and they aren't meeting them, it is your job to tell them. Not talking about it creates resentment—first your own resentment, because you will see them underperform or make a particular mistake several times. And second, holding off on giving feedback will eventually cause resentment in the employee. Why? Because eventually you *will* tell them how they are making a misstep, but after bottling it up for so long it's likely to come out a lot more harshly than you intended. Now the employee is angry you blew up at them or didn't share the feedback earlier.

If you are the kind of person who gets anxious about this, here are some examples you can adapt when you need to ask an employee to course correct in a direct but polite manner:

"Going forward, can you make sure to keep this door locked at all times? I'm worried about people gaining access when you have to step away."

"I'm looking to standardize how we handle the end-of-day closeout. Here's the checklist I want everyone to follow. Look it over and let me know if you have any questions or if anything comes up as you start to implement it."

"We've received feedback from our patrons that they stand in line too long. I want to go over some changes that I think could speed things up, but I also want to hear from you. Do you have any ideas that would improve our customer experience?"

"Please don't check your phone between customers. We want everyone to feel welcome when they approach you and this can feel unwelcoming. Put it down as soon as you see someone come to the door or save your phone for break times."

"I could do it better"

When you find an employee is not performing some task up to your expectations, you might find that you feel a twinge in the back of your mind. A feeling that whispers, "I could do that better." It can be hard to see an employee not meeting your expectations when you know you could do the job better.

What to do in this situation?

Please don't try to take the job over yourself. It might be tempting to think "Wouldn't it just be faster if I did it myself?" And maybe it would be in the moment! But that's not what you're paid for, and you have more important things to be doing. Here's the truth—there are probably plenty of tasks at the nonprofit that you would perform better than your employees. I'm not trying to belittle your employees. But it's true. The ED of a nonprofit brings a lot of experience and knowledge to any given task that your employees may not have. (In addition, you intuitively know how you want something to be done, and your employees aren't mind readers. So you will *always* have a leg up on your employees in that regard.)

But doing the job for your employee is a trap in the long run.

If you take over every task that you're better at, you'll triple your workload and won't be able to get the important work done. That means that you are going to have to develop ways to get your employees to perform at the level you expect.

The best option is simply to teach. Break down how and why you do a task a certain way and show your method to your employee, step by step. Showing the employee how you do something, combined with a perspective on why it's important, can really help.

Then pair this teaching with a system that helps the

employee succeed. Perhaps you give the employee an essential question or duty to be asked at the end of the task that she is struggling with. "Run every email through spell check" is a good way to help an employee send clearer communications. As long as she's done that, she's good. Will that catch her incorrect use of *its* or *it's*? Maybe not. But it should remove the worst offending typos. If the job is complex enough, you might consider a checklist. Something like: "Ten things to check before sending out the email newsletter."

Finally, you can serve as the review panel and ask any employee to run something by you, or another employee, before considering it complete. All of these steps are preferable to just you taking over a job yourself.

Instead of adding more to your plate, focus your skills in the areas where the nonprofit really needs your help—planning, fundraising, management, and more. If you do that, someday you will be able to afford to hire employees who can more often produce A+ work without this level of coaching by you. But you won't get there if you keep doing the job for your employees.

Accepting B+ work

Whether you think you could do the job better or not, sometimes the ED of a small nonprofit is simply going to have to settle for getting B+ work from employees instead of work worthy of an A+.

To give just one example of why this is the case, think about the employee I mentioned earlier—the young mother who works at a small nonprofit because she needs flexible work hours and wants to build her professional experience. You can't expect her to come into the nonprofit with every skill you need in the position. She's going to have to *learn* some of it. And that means you're going to have to teach—and let experience teach as well. That means, by default, her early work may not be up to your standards.

If you are on a small budget and hire someone with great potential, it's patently unfair to expect that person to be amazing at everything right out of the gate. You have to work with your employees! You have to model what you want and teach what you can. This process takes time.

And, even after all of that, you may still find that you wish you could get more from an employee than she can give. She might be solid at eighty percent of her duties, but continues to struggle with the other twenty percent. Sometimes, there are limitations on employees' skills—and your ability (and time) to teach. If you come up against these walls, where an employee just never gets to the level you need in certain areas, you're going to have to decide how important these tasks are.

If you're getting B+ work or better...then don't kill yourself trying to "fix" things to get someone to A+ work. At some point, you have to be willing to say, "The work I'm getting from this employee is good enough." I often say that "perfect is the enemy of the good." If you have a reasonably good employee, too much focus on the areas where she is not up to your standards will eventually be dispiriting and may waste a lot of hours of both your time.

Finding superpowers

It's important to point out that your employee doing B+ work probably has some areas where she could really shine. The marketing coordinator who struggles with typos when she writes the newsletter might make amazing videos for your nonprofit's social media channels. The program manager who is constantly disorganized might be amazing at building lasting relationships with your clientele that bring them back over and over again.

If you're not looking for these talents, you might miss them in your drive to "correct" their other work. The more you get to know your staff, the more you can seek these skills out. A place to start: simply ask them what they like to do and what they're good at. See where it takes you.

I will also note that in those cases where you find an employee is *really* good at something, lean into her superpower.

The marketing coordinator who makes amazing short videos on social media? Let her at it. Can she make a video for you every other week? Too often, managers only leverage these talents infrequently—once or twice a year around their "real" duties. No! You stumbled into having an amazing videographer and social media manager on your staff. Use her talents as much as possible.

The slightly disorganized program manager who forms such lasting bonds with your clientele that they keep coming back? Same thing—put her in a place where she can build that clientele one friendship at a time. Don't hide her away in the back office where she's only using her superpower by accident.

In both cases, you can shape the work and the organization to let your employees excel with their innate talents. You just have to look for them first.

Servant leadership

Servant leadership means using your power as ED to make the day-to-day experience of working at your nonprofit better. It puts your employees and volunteers first. This means identifying roadblocks in their job (such as bad software, outdated procedures, problem customers) and clearing them as best as you can. It means striving to find ways you can help them.

Consider a pilgrimage across a desert. The servant carries as many bags as possible, makes the tea, and starts the fire, while the ostensible "leader" focuses on the map. But if the servant should disappear, the journey would fall apart. (The novel *Journey to the East* by Hermann Hesse features a storyline like this, and it turns out that the servant was in fact the head of the religious group that sponsored the pilgrimage in the first place— he was the real leader all along, so the story goes. It's a story that features in almost every "servant leadership" book I've read.)

So if your employee is overloaded at the front desk, come up and ask, "What can I do to help?" Whether her answer is "deal with this angry customer" or "hand out name tags," you do it. In servant leadership, there's no such thing as a job that's "beneath you."

Join your staff stuffing envelopes with gusto (and joyful camaraderie) and you'll find the value of servant leadership.

And if you are wondering how this squares with my above admonition not to take over the work of your employee, here's my answer. Servant leadership *does not* mean that you are doing the job of the employee. Relieving your employee of a duty when they are stressed and overwhelmed is a true help. Spending a little time being part of the team feels good—for them and you. You are helping and building trust. Doing their job for them communicates distrust and maybe even arrogance. It's a subtle distinction but an important one.

Team captain

In addition to managing individuals, you are also a manager of the overall team.

When you have two or more employees, a big part of the responsibility is managing the normal difficulties of interpersonal relationships. "George isn't helping with my project," Alice says. "Alice asks for everything last minute," George says. And they are both looking at you to sort it out! Fun, eh?

Most of the time, you'll be able to sort these out pretty easily. Both George and Alice could probably do better working together and you can cajole, order, and lead them to work these out. In particular, look for opportunities to build systems centered around:

- *Communication*, such as using group chat tools as opposed to massive reply-all chains.
- *Resource sharing*, such as a staff Intranet (at the time of writing there are many free or very cheap options) to host internal documents and processes that everyone needs.
- *Checklists*, such as a standardized way to open the gift shop every morning and close down every night, no matter who the employee is.
- *Regular meetings*, with a focus on making them short and on-topic, can be useful for reporting between members of staff, while longer and infrequent free-flowing meetings can help spur new ideas. Try to keep them separate or you will meeting your staff to death.

All of these tools help make sure that information flows between members of the organization *without you being a bottleneck*.

Finally, you have an obligation to keep your employees physically safe and free from harassment. Conditions that create an unsafe workplace (whether those are toxic people or just dangerous pieces of equipment) need your highest drop-everything-and-deal-with-this-now priority if something goes wrong. But instead of having to respond to an emergency, spend the time *in advance* to stop issues from happening.

Don't view sexual harassment training, workshop safety training, antibullying training, or anything like those examples as things that take away from "the real work." It's much better, and it takes less time, to go through the trainings than to manage the fallout of the consequences of *not* doing the trainings.

Turnover

When it comes to staff, an Executive Director of a small nonprofit has one big threat we need to address at length —turnover.

Let's start with a crucial question: Why is turnover a problem at small nonprofits in particular? The main reason: larger nonprofits have enough people in place to preserve institutional knowledge during staff changes. If a private high school has a development department of eight people, they will be able to replace employees without losing too much during the transitions. Why? Because when one person leaves, the seven remaining people can tell the new employee how things work. They know the rules, the culture, and the relationships. So transitions aren't as hard. If the new major gifts officer gets a call from someone who (for whatever reason) isn't in their database, they can ask around the office and find more information.

Compare that to a small nonprofit where a single person often handles all the duties of an entire department at a larger organization. When these small nonprofits lose a development staffer...that staffer might be the only one. This time, when the new staffer gets off the phone with the donor and asks around the office, "What do you know about this donor?" they are much more likely to get a lot of blank stares from the program person and the education person, who don't know anything about the development side of the house.

At a small nonprofit, the newbie is starting over from scratch. And this happens every time there's turnover in a position. Things get lost in the shuffle and it's as if each new hire is re-creating their positions all over again. This cycle repeats over and over, and right there you have a primary reason some small nonprofits can never quite get their feet under them.

An ED can address this in two main ways. The most obvious is preventing the reasons for turnover as best as possible (more on this in the next section). The second is by working as hard as possible to alleviate the effects of turnover. This can involve using technology and databases to document systems and information (the Four Ds!). Active management of employees will help as well, because the ED will be more familiar with the job and can guide the new employee. And cross-training of staff can help too.

Preventing turnover

Turnover happens for a variety of reasons. Some of it is unavoidable—retirement or a cross-country move. That's not the kind of turnover you can usually do anything about. So some level of staff turnover is to be expected. But turnover can happen for reasons that you might actually be able to address, such as staff members who leave because they want to make more money, pursue an opportunity for more professional development, or escape a bad work environment.

Fighting turnover can be hard. Let's consider again the

example early in this chapter—a mother in her thirties who loves the work, wants flexibility, and wants professional experience. As her need for flexibility lessens as her kids get older, she's going to want either more money or more professional experience. Can your nonprofit give her either of those?

It is entirely likely that you can't easily boost her pay much. Small nonprofits as a whole usually pay below market versus larger nonprofits or for-profit businesses. This is especially true during a booming labor market. When wages are rising, staff eventually figure out that they could make more money (sometimes a lot more money) elsewhere. We'll talk more about money in the next chapter, and I have a separate book in this series about fundraising, *The Little Book of Gold: Fundraising for Small (and Very Small) Nonprofits*, that might also help increase your revenue and thus boost your ability to pay employees closer to what they're worth.

But there are other options you can offer.

What about more professional experience? Are there new projects she can tackle? New ways to stay engaged? The challenge here is that this kind of work often goes along with a new title, and that often goes along with a raise. Some nonprofits choose to give just the title increase instead. And so the program coordinator becomes the program manager...the program manager becomes the program director. Title inflation is common in small nonprofits for precisely this reason—an Executive Director wants to keep an employee and rewards them with a better title (but often not a commensurate pay increase).

In general, if you can give meaningful work to someone *without* inflating their title (unless you can also increase pay at the same time) you'll do better in the long run. The cynical reason for this is that, in some ways, the title inflation just makes it *easier* for someone to get hired elsewhere. After all, program director will look better on a résumé than program manager.

But a title change without more pay or more resources to work with is also not necessarily great for the employee either. Along with title changes, there is usually an increase in expectations and responsibility. If you also haven't increased the resources available to that person to manage, or paid them more to make it worthwhile, what you've done is just add to their stress load.

So, varied and meaningful work is important for retention, to whatever degree your operations can allow. Letting the employee chart her own course will help as well. If the ideas for her new project come from both of you *together*, you have a better chance to keep her.

Workplace environment

Keeping your employees engaged with their work is just part of the retention question. There's one thing you're really going to want to get right to prevent turnover—workplace environment. If the job is miserable because of high stress, annoying coworkers, or a micromanaging boss (AKA you), then they are much more likely to leave. If coming into work on a Monday morning feels like a drag to them, your employees are going to look for a new place to work, and sooner rather than later.

People can put up with low wages for a long time if they believe their work is important and they love coming into the office. But if it's soul-sucking, well, why spend a third of their day in a place that doesn't feel good? They'll eventually leave.

"The Flexibility Trap"

This sets up what I think about as "The Flexibility Trap" at small nonprofits.

Here's the trap: On the one hand, to retain employees, an ED wants to be flexible and work with the employees to accommodate them. On the other hand, in an effort to retain their employees, EDs can let their staff go overboard. And so one employee's flexibility becomes another employee's daily frustration.

"Oh, you need to leave early to get your kids? Ok!" leads to...

"Oh, you want to have your dog at your desk? Ok..." leads to...

"Oh, you want your dog *and* your kids at your desk with you? For all of summer break? Well...um...hmm...ok, I guess we can work with that..." leads to...

"Oh, your coworkers are complaining that you're being rude to them when they ask you about your work? Well, listen, try to be kinder if you can. I'll talk to them about giving you some space to get things done."

By this point, though, the message you are sending to the employee is actually "Whatever you do, *don't leave!*"

The *fear* of employees leaving can be just as damaging to a nonprofit as the employees actually leaving, because it can set up a terrible workplace culture that drives away everyone else but the one or two employees you are terrified to lose.

It can end up creating a situation where a small nonprofit has one or two people who have been there seemingly forever, while every other position is filled by someone who rarely stays more than a year or two—driven out by the difficulties of working with the two people who think they are invulnerable to consequences of bad behavior (and who the ED treats as if they are invulnerable).

Getting out of the Flexibility Trap

The first temptation of some EDs is to avoid the Flexibility Trap by running their small nonprofit like the military. They offer little to no flexibility and expect punctuality and strict rules. From everything I've seen, this sets up an untenable situation.

I love *systems*. But strict *rules* are different, and at small nonprofits they don't take into account the fact that the organization is fundamentally fragile. (Whereas something like the military is much more resilient, with significant resources behind it.)

A focus on punctuality may work most of the time...until there's an issue at daycare, or a missed bus, or an aging parent who needs help. If you don't have a decent wage to go with the strict rules, the choice you are offering employees is this—low pay on the one hand or taking care of essential life problems on the other hand. They won't choose you.

To be clear: focusing on extreme punctuality may be necessary in some situations. Rules and checklists have their place when safety is on the line. But even in life and death situations —such as flying planes or performing surgery—the true breakthroughs in safety went beyond the checklist to improving the communications and changing the culture of the cockpit and operating room. (If you are operating in a high-risk environment you should investigate "crew resource management," the communications system that has been adopted by all airlines and is increasingly adopted elsewhere when lives are on the line.)

A fast food restaurant can use its extreme focus on rules, systems, and punctuality because they know there is a vast workforce waiting for those jobs. If a current employee can't be bothered to show up on time, well, there's a line of potential employees who would like the chance. But show me the line of (qualified) people queueing up to be an underpaid employee at a small nonprofit dealing with some of the most challenging problems in the country. I'll wait.

I recommend not trying to get out of the Flexibility Trap this way.

The solution to avoiding the Flexibility Trap is actually a fairly simple two-step process. First, recognize that it exists! As with many problems, that's an important first step. And second, *be flexible with your staff in as many ways as you can, but not with behavior that affects others at the nonprofit.* Bad or disruptive behavior is not worth tolerating just to keep someone around because you are afraid to lose their institutional knowledge.

Variable schedules, leaving early to get kids, a midday dentist appointment, working from home one day a week...all this can be worked out. In fact, there are studies that show job satisfaction is highly correlated to the feeling of control over one's schedule more than almost any other factor.

But can you trust them to get their work done even in these situations? Yes, mostly. When the request for an allowance is made, I find it effective to state the reason why you're accommodating the request. "It's fine if you need to pick your kids up early, I trust that you'll make up the time later this week." Or: "I know you always put in extra time—you don't have to check with me on doctor's appointments, just schedule them when it works for you." Or: "I have no problem with you trying out working from home on Fridays. Your work is always solid and if that continues, I have no problem with it."

In each case, you are implicitly making a contract with the person. The employee will appreciate your trust and also remember that they shouldn't break it. This is better than a "do what you want" alternative where they feel like you're not watching at all. And it's also likely better than an explicit message to them. Don't try: "You can try working from home on Fridays but I'm going to watch for any slippage in your work quality." That's not the same thing! Reaffirm the positives of their work and the trust in your relationship, as opposed to framing it as a threat.

Of course, sometimes your nonprofit is structured in such a way that it is very difficult to be able to grant an employee's request for an allowance. If a receptionist asks to leave every day at 3:30 to go pick up her kids after school, you might feel like it's an impossibility. "I'm sorry, I wish I could make that work. But we simply aren't set up to accommodate it. Clients have meetings scheduled all the way until five o'clock and with our secure entrance, we need someone there. Maybe there are some other ways we can be flexible, though."

Perhaps the front desk could close at 3:30 and the rest of the staff could buzz people in through the door for the remainder of the day. Or maybe the receptionist could leave the desk unstaffed for a half hour while she gets her kids and brings them back to the office to let them do their homework quietly in a conference room? You are a small nonprofit—look for ways to say yes, so long as it doesn't overly affect your other staff members!

But if you truly can't say yes, then you're going to have to say so, and make it clear you are open to other ways to accommodate your employee. It happens. Be gracious and do your best to find something that works for both of you. She will appreciate your effort.

Pulling back from too-flexible options

If you've already granted flexibility to an employee that you have now come to regret, you may need to rescind it, *especially* if it's affecting other people's work environment. In general, you should avoid this situation when possible, but if you've made an allowance—or if your predecessor did—and that now needs to be changed, here are some quick ideas on how to approach it.

Talk to the employee one-on-one and report that the situation isn't working. Don't throw any of your other employees under the bus. "George said it's disruptive to have your toddler in the office every day" is a sure way to cause a rift between your employees. You can state that the situation is a problem without breaking confidence. For example: "Watching things over the last few weeks, I've observed that it's become a much more difficult work environment when your son is in the office."

As before, go into the conversation looking for ways to accommodate the employee's needs. For example: "Would your son be willing to spend the last hour of the day doing homework in the conference room or watching TV instead of having free access to the rest of the building?" Or: "Would you be able to structure your work so that you could work from home for the last hour of the day and watch your son there?" Or: "Could you come in early each morning so that you can clock out at 3:30 instead of 5:00?"

Looking for new ways to accommodate the employee's needs are important here because they will have a sense that there's a broken promise either from you or your predecessor. And it's especially important if we're talking about things that could have a dramatic impact on someone's finances. An employee having a child in the office every afternoon might be frustrating for some, but the only alternative for that employee may be childcare that costs them several hundred dollars a month. And even if they were able to pay it, it might not be available right away.

As before, it's also possible that there's an issue that just can't be accommodated—that, in your view, the request has reached a breaking point and to continue it would be risking too much. In that case, you will have to be blunt. "I'm sorry that we can't keep making this accommodation. I can give you another week or two to sort out alternate arrangements, but it's become too big a distraction to let it go on any longer."

Staff behaving badly

Finally, I can hear you asking about how to handle employees who want flexibility or some special allowance that would be technically workable but that you just don't want to grant. "But what if I *could* make an allowance for this employee's request, but I don't want to, because I don't trust them?" The answer is simple: then don't grant it.

If you don't trust that your employee will actually get work done if they work from home on Fridays, let's say, then I'll change the focus: you have an employee you don't trust. That's a much bigger deal than just addressing whether they can work from home on Friday.

Let's spend a moment talking about how you can intervene when employees need a course correction.

Correcting employee behavior

If you have an employee who has stepped over a line or is not pulling their weight, you need to have a conversation with them. Here are some tips for making sure that goes well:

Close the door.

Praise your employees in front of others, but save the corrective conversations for one-on-one meetings. Don't dress them down in front of others. It can be humiliating for the employee and embarrassing for the people who have to watch it. (The exception to this is if you directly witness harassing or other highly inappropriate behavior. It's good to call it out in the moment, but save the corrective conversation for later: "Tim, that's not an appropriate comment in the workplace. I'm going to close the staff meeting early. Meet me in my office in five minutes.")

Be clear about what you're talking about.

As a manager, you owe it to the employee to be clear about the problem. If you're going to make an employee sit through an awkward conversation, clarity will help you both. If you are conflict-averse, this might be hard for you, and you may be tempted to talk around the problem and build up to it. That's not the right way to go. Before you have the conversation, work out your opening line and address the problem right up front. "I need to talk to you about last night's event. Some of our donors complained that it wasn't up to our usual standards, and I'd like to explore with you how we can improve the event experience." Or "I know we have a flexible workplace, but I still need you to show up on time to our staff meetings. It's wasteful of other people's time to make them wait for everyone to show up."

Focus on the behavior, not the person.

When you are frustrated with an employee's behavior, it can be tempting to generalize in a way that makes it sound like you are attacking them as a person. "You're always late to meetings" can sound like an attack. Whereas "I need you to come to staff meetings on time" is clear and focused on the behavior (not the person). "Do you understand basic grammar?" is much, *much* worse than "I need you to spend more time polishing your emails to our partners."

. . .

Correct, then praise.

You may also have the temptation to build someone up *before* you try to correct their behavior. But if you do it this way, they will start to expect the other shoe to drop whenever you praise them! Instead, first talk to them about their behavior, talk about ways to correct it, and then—when you feel like you are both on the same page—spend some time praising them: "Thank you for having that conversation. I'm glad we're on the same page about the event and I think we have some good ideas about how to make sure it doesn't happen again. I think so highly of your work and your dedication. You are a star on the team and I'm so glad I get to work with you."

———

Linda wanted to start making some changes. She considered sitting her employees down for an annual review (in the first year that she'd been there, she hadn't done one for either employee yet). But she decided against it. She thought it would feel like she was unloading on them with a year's worth of grievances. Instead she decided to pick just one area to focus on with each.

When her membership coordinator sent a newsletter with several mistakes in it, Linda called her into the office and told her that the mistakes would cause confusion for members and that they really needed a better system to make sure the details in the newsletter were correct. They decided that the membership coordinator would send the newsletter to both Linda and the bookkeeper before it went out and that she would follow up with both of them to make sure they had reviewed it.

That went pretty well!

Later, when Linda brought receipts to the bookkeeper, and the bookkeeper let out a sigh of frustration (or contempt? Linda wasn't sure) Linda called her out on the spot. "I know this isn't exactly how you would like the information presented but that response is inappropriate. Come into my office or send me an email if you have questions, but don't make a big thing about me not filling out the form. There's nothing that says you can't do that and bring it to me for a signature."

The bookkeeper seemed shocked. Linda felt pretty shocked that she'd even said it and she instantly wondered whether her frustration had gotten the best of her. It was difficult and awkward for both of them, but they eventually got through it. But she didn't get any more dramatic sighs when she brought her receipts to the bookkeeper anymore. That was a win.

A note on annual reviews

Some nonprofits conduct annual reviews of their employees, though in my experience most small nonprofits don't have things together enough to make them happen. Most likely, you'll do better to focus on regular interactions and small doses of feedback like I recommend above. *Don't* save up everything for the annual review. In general, whatever you include in the review should not surprise the employee. If an issue is important enough to bring it up during an annual review, it's important enough to give them direct feedback closer to the time the issue happens.

If I had to choose between annual reviews and regular performance feedback, I would opt for regular feedback every time.

Trying to manage employees through policy and employee handbooks

It also might be tempting to make a rule for every behavior you don't like. As organizations get larger and larger, their employee handbook gets thicker and thicker. Expansive employment policies make sense for large organizations. They are protecting themselves and they are protecting the employees.

It's less practical for a small nonprofit. First, creating these documents takes a lot of work. Often they are passed by the board of directors, which adds another complication to the process. Maintaining them is also a lot of work. As state or federal law changes, your employee policies might need to change too.

I'm not *against* these documents. They can be useful places to collect policies and procedures around vacation days, sick leave, and things like that. They can also be a place to house things like whistleblower policies or other things that seem relevant to your specific organization.

But don't rely on policies and handbooks to ensure your employees are using common sense. Consider the employee who says: "I'm really sorry it broke, but to be fair, you never said that I *couldn't* bring an ant farm into the office." You don't need a policy about bringing ant farms into the office! You are hiring employees for (among other things) their judgment, and it was poor judgment to bring an ant farm into the office. You can't create a policy for every situation, so don't try to use it as a crutch for actually managing your staff.

Employees are assets, not liabilities

While we're talking about correcting employee behavior, I'd like to interrupt for a moment to remind you that, in general, your employees are valuable and they should be treated as assets to the organization, not liabilities.

It's easy to think of the employees as *costs*. When you look at a budget, a huge amount of your expenses are undoubtedly related to staffing. So it's understandable that you might see only the high expense of having employees. But they are assets —and for many small nonprofits, they are the *only* assets.

Consider what I said at the top of the chapter—that turnover is one of the biggest problems with managing a small nonprofit staff. If that's true, then it follows that the opposite is true too—keeping good employees (as well as their relationships, skills, and knowledge) is incredibly valuable to the nonprofit.

So let's treat employees this way! How do you treat personal assets? Do you wash your car and take it in for regular mainte-nance? Do you spend time and money to improve your home, even when you don't "have to?" Please do these same things with your employees. Treat them well, honor their work, and they will treat you well and improve the nonprofit.

Even for Linda, who has two employees who at times frus-trate her, it's best to work to improve them as employees. Her employees might not be as valuable assets as she wished they were, but they are still assets to the organization.

This was an extended interruption, but a reminder about the true value of your employees is an important baseline for what comes next.

What if an employee's behavior isn't improving?

So you've been through the steps above to work with your employee. But nothing's improving. Or maybe it's even gotten worse because the employee is upset and is resisting you. Let's walk through how to deal with this situation.

First, call your board president!

In these situations, I'd start by informing your board president or the full executive committee. It is *firmly* up to you, and not the board, how to handle this employee. But one of my cardinal rules of being an ED is that you shouldn't surprise your board chair. A heads-up about any employment change of anyone on staff is a good idea, but it's an especially good idea if you think you are on a path that might result in having to fire someone.

The danger of doing this is that you might discover your board president has hang-ups you weren't aware of. If she was fired unfairly in the past, she might not want to see it repeated again and she will counsel extra caution. Or her job might be in a very different work environment—a university, for example— where she expects certain procedures to be followed and may be alarmed that your small nonprofit doesn't have the same procedures in place.

You can't always know these things in advance, so you can judge by your relationship. The stronger the relationship, the more likely you can probably trust that giving a heads-up is enough. If you aren't sure how she will react, then you'd do better to tell the entire executive committee.

Research state law

You can find resources online—either from your state or from business websites such as a chamber of commerce—that will give you an overview on employee termination. There may be things you can and can't do. Learn the rules in advance.

Gently probe your other employees

It is inappropriate to gossip with your employees about other employees. But if you've observed problematic behavior, or heard a report of it, then it's possible that there is other behavior you are unaware of. In these cases, it's ok to inquire. During a routine one-on-one meeting, you might ask an employee how the team is doing. "How are you working with your fellow coworkers?" We are taught from an early age not to tattle, so it's likely your employees will answer questions like this with platitudes that don't really tell you much. Don't stop there, though. For example, you can follow up your question with, "I can't go into any detail, but I hear that working with Tim has been more difficult lately. Have you experienced anything like that?"

It's a simple question, and you will either get nothing in reply or something very specific. If an employee has seen problem behavior, they might not be willing to volunteer it when you posed a general question. But if you specifically *ask*, things might be different.

They also might not have experienced anything worth reporting. Either way, don't linger on it. Thank them and ask that they keep the conversation confidential.

Plan for the worst

You are about to have a difficult conversation with a staff member. Hopefully you can resolve it. If you can't, you may decide you need to fire this employee or they may quit suddenly after your meeting. Who will step in? Can you fill in with current staff? Could volunteers help? A temp? Knowing what you might do in advance is worth the effort. I have had to terminate people in key positions (like a volunteer coordinator managing hundreds of volunteers) and I wasn't willing to move forward until I had identified who I was going to ask in the short term to step in.

As part of this, you also need to do a quick inventory of access to systems and technology you need to keep track of as well (laptops, passwords, keycards, etc.). Again, it's good to be prepared for the worst outcome.

The last chance meeting

At this point you've either seen problematic behavior or you've heard it reported (and possibly corroborated). So what now? The main question is whether you think the situation is egregious enough to simply take action or whether you want to give the employee a final chance to change their behavior. You might take into consideration whether there's an established pattern of behavior, the severity of the behavior, and even how crucial the work of the problem employee is to the organization (though this is the least of the factors).

If you do want to take action now, we'll deal with actual termination below.

But let's say you are *not* ready to fire a problem employee at this point. You do want to give her one more shot to mend her ways. That's what this "last chance meeting" is for (this is also commonly known as a "come to Jesus meeting" but I think it's easier to talk about if we leave him out of it).

The main goal for this meeting is to communicate one essential fact: this behavior must stop...or else. You can have "or else" be stated or unstated, but it should be clear. The message is: you see this happening, and it needs to stop. No ifs, ands, or buts. "Your commenting on Jan's appearance and clothing is inappropriate for the workplace and it must stop immediately. This is nonnegotiable, Tim."

Importantly, this conversation should not become an *argu-*

ment over the facts. *Listen*, if need be. There might be something there that changes your view. Or, there might be something there that just makes you madder. But, again, I recommend against arguing back. Once you start arguing, you're tacitly accepting the premise that if they win the argument, they didn't do something wrong. Don't take the bait. Stay cool and collected. The behavior must stop.

Keep it short. Give the employee the rest of the day off to think about it. The goal is a jolt to the employee. If they've been coasting along, assuming they are invulnerable or that their behavior is fine, this meeting is the wake-up call. It's on them to decide if they will listen.

The final step

As I hope I've made clear, the fear of losing an employee can hold back a nonprofit just as much as actually losing employees from turnover. Because sometimes it has to happen.

The first time I ever fired someone, I was twenty-four. The employee was an older man, maybe older than my dad. His title was volunteer coordinator and he managed hundreds of volunteers. It was a huge job. And I was getting reports that things weren't working as they should.

For all my writing above about dealing with "problem employees" and all that...it wasn't the case here. The nonprofit relied on its volunteers and getting complaints from volunteers and staff for such a key role made me feel that the job was too important to let the situation fester longer. After I decided it was time, and got my ducks in a row as described above, I called a meeting with the volunteer coordinator, and I had my first line ready to go. I recommend something similar in my book on fundraising when it comes to making the ask—the same principle applies here. Memorizing an important sentence is good preparation.

"Tim, I've come to the conclusion that I have to let you go."

That was my line. I've used that line every other time I've had to fire an employee.

(And his name also wasn't Tim, to be clear.)

It sucks to deliver. And, of course, it sucks more to hear—don't let yourself be fooled by how hard it is to fire someone. You're not the story.

Don't go overboard with regret and praise to try to build up the employee. That's just gaslighting. If you felt that way, you wouldn't be doing this. Don't be cruel. And, as above, *don't get into an argument*. The time for arguments is done. Don't be baited.

Kindly ask for anything back that you need. Ask for passwords, keys, and anything else. Let the employee clean out her desk and stay close, but don't loom over her like you think she is going to take things that don't belong to her (unless that is the reason for her termination).

And escort her to the door with a farewell.

Ideally, that moment should be the last moment the employee works for your organization. Don't try to ask them to work beyond the time they know they have been fired. Sometimes this can work in situations of layoffs, but I wouldn't try it here. If you have the finances to swing it, I also recommend paying at least two weeks to a month of salary or regular hours after the date of firing. (You should have these terms ready to go before the process occurs.) Even if this is not legally required in your state, it makes this pill a little easier to swallow.

Again—it's not a fun process. Doing it well doesn't mean it feels any better.

But that first employee I fired that I told you about? The volunteer coordinator? When I walked him to the door, I said goodbye to him and watched him go. I turned back inside feeling uncertain. Were we ready to do this without him? Could we cover the duties until a new person was in the spot? At that moment, a volunteer asked where he was going and I told her that I'd let him go. Her reaction totally caught me off guard: she *hugged* me. Because, as a volunteer, she'd seen all the same problems and had her own real frustrations with the volunteer coordinator as well.

It was a meaningful moment for me, and an important reminder. If you have to take this step, remember that you are doing it to protect the organization and to protect the employee's coworkers. Those coworkers, your other employees (and volunteers in my case), are watching. They know there's a problem—in fact, they've probably known longer than you. How you handle it will determine a lot.

Let's hire!

With all of that out of the way, let's turn to one of the best parts of leading a nonprofit: hiring. Hiring a new employee is one of the most powerful ways to make change at your nonprofit.

If you are brought on to lead a nonprofit with existing staff, then the chance to hire your first new employee will be especially meaningful. Your new employee will be the first who doesn't remember the old boss or how things used to be. To the new employee, you're the boss and always have been.

But how do you find the right person to fill your need? Whether you are filling an existing position or creating a new one, here are some questions to think about before you start advertising a position.

Do you truly need to hire (or rehire)?

If someone has recently left their position, it's often tempting to try to get someone in to fill the exact same job immediately. But before you do that, really look at how your organization works without the position. It's possible that you can make something work with existing staff, and you may not know until you try. If you've already created opportunities for cross-training within the organization, this will be easier to try. The goal is to watch your staff (and yourself) and evaluate what works and what doesn't.

Let's say you lose someone who had a full-time position. If you split up their duties among three employees and yourself for a month or two, you will be able to evaluate how it works. If it doesn't work, no worries: hire the position again. If it does work, you now have some real space in your budget to get the remaining employees up to a better pay.

And if it only partially works—let's say most of the duties can be divided up well, but some others just keep falling through the cracks—now you have an opportunity to make an interesting change. You can hire a new full-time employee who has a lot of the same duties but also some new ones, expanding your organizational capacity. Or you might be able to give some of those remaining duties to a new part-time employee and build in more flexibility and resilience to the organization.

The point is—you may not know until you try. If you leave a position unfilled for a short window of time to test it, you'll get the opportunity to find out.

What's the job?

If you do need to hire, the real question is: What kind of position do you need filled? Small nonprofits often hire with a similar hierarchy of titles no matter their sector—coordinator, manager, director. For example: a program coordinator, a program manager, a program director. I think it's a reasonable framework. Here's a rough guide to the work at each title level:

- A *coordinator* is task-oriented, and the tasks are usually determined by the person above her. This position likely supports the team internally and rarely works outside the organization. Titles might look something like this: program coordinator, development coordinator, marketing coordinator...
- A *manager* is usually strong enough at her job that she can manage her own time, a complex project, a program, or other people. Managers don't have to manage other people, but they certainly can, depending on the size of your organization. Someone with the manager title is more likely to work with people outside the organization. Titles might look something like this: annual fund manager, membership manager, marketing manager...
- A *director*, almost by default, should oversee other staff members. While a manager may not have people who report to her, a director usually should. This person is doing more than managing people. She is leading a team toward growth and big goals. She is making big decisions within her respective realm, almost at the same level as the Executive Director. Titles might look something like this: director of operations, director of development, finance director...

Think about the kind of work you need done and compare

it to this breakdown of titles. It should help you get the right kind of position hired.

Hire from the bottom up

A common problem in nonprofits is to hire "too high" along that hierarchy. So for an ED of a small nonprofit who feels like she can never get a handle on fundraising, the temptation is to hire a director of development. But if there's no budget for other development staff to report to that new position, then it's not the right hire. You should start hiring from the bottom up.

Why? It's not just because the director of development "should" have people to supervise. I'm not advocating this because of a theoretical chain of command or anything like that. My suggestions in this regard are actually practical and economical. Here's what tends to happen when you hire someone to be the director of development (or any other director level position) without the supporting staff and infrastructure.

A director of development—based on my notes about the kinds of responsibilities you should expect from a director-level position—should be a decision maker, a strategic thinker, and a leader. But without the resources of managers and coordinators who work for them, what do they most often do? The menial tasks! The highly paid director of development you just hired will handle grant writing, gift processing, database work, hundreds of small gifts, and envelope stuffing. That work will consume her day and she will never get to the big opportunities like cultivation of major donors. The end result is that you *overpay* for work that a development coordinator could have done eighty percent of, while getting few of the benefits of having a director of development.

Here's another way to think about the problem of hiring too high up the org chart:

Imagine that Linda wants to build a full development department. What might that look like? She sketches out a list. A director of development, a major gifts officer, an annual fund manager, an events manager, a grant writer, and a development coordinator. (Note—this team could raise millions, so it's overkill for most small nonprofits. The point of the exercise is to imagine what the department *could* look like if it were built out like a robust organization.) Linda has a membership coordinator right now, but besides that she is doing everything on the org chart. Maybe she's doing all of them at only ten or twenty percent of what could be done, but at some point during the year, she will wear all those hats. If she hires a development director, now *that* person's name is on every position on the org chart. She didn't really change much.

But when you hire from the bottom up, you are hiring a new position at a rate of pay that makes sense for the job, and you are relieving a lot of hours from your own plate. Again, a lot of the job at the top is decision-making and leadership. Linda is already doing that! So she should hire someone to help with the things that are eating away from her *time*.

The ED of a small nonprofit experiencing growth in its fundraising might first hire a development coordinator, then an annual fund manager, and then a grant writer before hiring a full-time director of development. (The specifics of the positions would of course vary by the nonprofit.) But the point stands. You will spend less of your budget and get more of what you actually want if you hire from the bottom up.

Hiring based on a candidate's potential

It is common at nonprofits to hire people who are likely to excel in the position but who don't have the documented job experience to actually prove it. Someone just out of college, a young parent returning to the workforce, or a senior looking to do something different with their last few years in the workforce may all be good candidates for a job but don't have the résumé to back it up.

I've written something similar already, but now we get to deal with the question: *How* do you know if someone has this kind of potential?

The first thing to look for is nontraditional experience. For example, someone who has never held a *job* throwing events, but throws amazing house parties, might be a great event planner, even if she never held the title anywhere. Someone who has never had a job raising money, but has served on the auction committee at their child's school for the last five years, might be a good fundraiser. Don't discount volunteer or personal experience. Similarly, there are "transferable skills" between jobs that don't seem to have anything in common at first glance. A retired librarian might make a great development coordinator because both jobs involve a lot of time working with databases. It's not always obvious, but many kinds of skills can transfer into new contexts.

You can also "test" for skills. If you've never hired before, you might not know that this is an option. But if you have a candidate who you'd like to hire, but aren't sure about certain skills, you can ask a candidate (or all your finalists) to demonstrate something. When applying for a job leading marketing, one nonprofit gave me a preview of their new brand and asked me and two other finalists to present to them on how I would roll it out. That's appropriate for a high-level position. But for jobs with titles like coordinator you can ask candidates to complete simple tasks. You might, for example, present an email from a donor. Give them the key information about the donor and the topic and then give them time to write a response. This kind of exercise will tell you *so much* about a candidate's potential.

Hiring people like yourself

Earlier we talked about how a wise ED can look for staff to balance out their own strengths and weaknesses. This all sounds well and good until we get to the actual selection. That's when the temptation to hire someone you like more than someone who is qualified rears its head. It's tempting to hire people who you would like to be your friend. But your organization needs an actual good employee, not just someone who you'd like to get a beer with. Don't let this temptation override the rest of the search process.

It's also tempting to hire someone who has a similar kind of shared experience as you. For example: "I went to Smallville College and it helped prepare me for the working world, so this candidate who also went to Smallville College is probably ready too." It might feel like it tracks, but it actually often doesn't work this way. This kind of shared connection shouldn't be enough to paper over a lack of qualifications or experience. I went to a high school and a college with very strong networks of alumni. I think of those networks as good ways to open a door and to maybe even get an interview. But they shouldn't be reason enough on their own to offer a job.

Again, look for a demonstration or evidence of the skills you need. Not just a shared background or story.

Beware of offering the job because you want to help the person applying

Potential is great, but a nonprofit ED needs to make sure she isn't trying to *help* the applicant more than her own organization. I've seen something like this happen often enough at small nonprofits that I think it's worth calling attention to.

Here's the problem: nonprofit leaders want to help people. Isn't this why we work at nonprofits after all? But this line can get blurred in the hiring process. You might see a candidate who seems like she's had a run of really hard luck. Someone who could *really* use this job.

So you hire her to give her a leg up, and that's when you discover that she is wildly unsuited for the position, because your desire to help overrode your assessment of her actual qualifications. This ends poorly, and with bad blood all around. So I'll reiterate what I said above: if a candidate doesn't have certain experience on her résumé, you can look for other ways to see if she is qualified. But be wary if you feel that you want to hire someone *despite* her lack of qualifications. That's a sign that you are trying to help her more than she can help you and your organization.

Help people through the work of your mission. If you are also trying to help people by offering them jobs and then end up with someone who doesn't have the ability to do the job you hired her for, you are hurting the people you serve.

Hiring someone "overqualified"

This is the flip side of the above caution.

Some candidates may apply for a junior position that they are overqualified for. I'm talking about situations where someone who was once a director of marketing for a large company applies for a junior marketing job at a small nonprofit. This is subtly different from someone who was highly qualified in a *different* field, such as the same former director of marketing who takes an early retirement and decides they want to give back and be a social worker.

But if someone overqualified applies for your position, it creates a tricky situation. No matter what the candidate says, it's hard not to wonder if there is a skeleton in her closet somewhere preventing her from taking a better-paying job.

Even in the best of scenarios, that candidate may eventually start to resent that she doesn't have more responsibility and more opportunities to use her talents. A skilled development professional who says she wants a job doing database work will eventually spot opportunities where she could use her expertise to help the situation. Which might seem great at first—after all you are getting significant experience at a bargain rate. But as she takes on more responsibilities commensurate with her ability, who will do the database work that still needs to be done?

If you have reason to believe that you are a growing organization and will be able to provide new opportunities for this person, this might work out. And it is possible that this person is truly content to have a task-oriented job because she doesn't want to take the job home with her anymore, or any number of reasons why someone would want a relatively simple job. But, most of the time, you will do better to hire a candidate who is well-suited for the actual job you are hiring for, and not the person qualified to be her boss (or your boss!).

Volunteers

Some nonprofits rely on volunteers for their operations—they wouldn't survive without them. Other nonprofits rarely use volunteers—perhaps just as extra staffing at special events.

There's no one right model for every nonprofit.

When handled correctly, volunteers can augment your organization and can improve your reach and service without the cost of an employee.

In general, you should think of two different kinds of volunteer models. The first is "shift work." At the Grand Cinema, we had a couple hundred volunteers who filled shifts in the movie theater—selling concessions, taking tickets, cleaning theaters. Every day we were open, two or three shifts of volunteers did these jobs in exchange for a free movie ticket at the end of the shift. It was an incredible system.

You see this in a variety of places. A soup kitchen, for example, may have shifts of volunteers who come in to prepare and then serve meals. Or a nonprofit asks mentors to work with at-risk youth on certain evenings of the week. The key point is that the organization is asking volunteers to work for a limited period of time with a narrowly defined scope of work.

This model rewards clear expectations and regular training. Even though the work is fairly basic, your volunteers will excel if you have a system for training new volunteers and retraining long-time volunteers on new techniques.

The second model I like for volunteers is using individual volunteers for skilled project work.

I once had a volunteer I worked with for months on a big project. She was interested in the organization, approached us about volunteering her particular skills, and after some back-and-forth, we decided she should be an assistant on a massive five-day event. I was glad to have someone to help with such a big project. And she felt good about giving back. This kind of volunteer work is specific to the individual. It was work that was tailored to her skills and the needs of our organization.

This kind of model is also best if it has a natural end point. And if it doesn't, you should create one. I counsel something similar for volunteering on a nonprofit board by recommending terms. Volunteers can eventually feel trapped in a position if there's no clear place for their work to end. (I've been updating my church's website for the last twelve years because I never set up a clear end point, so I speak from experience here!)

Between shift work and skilled project work there exists a difficult middle ground—where too many volunteers are given skilled work that may be beyond them. It's demoralizing for the volunteers to feel like they aren't succeeding, it adds more time to the staff member trying to manage the volunteers, and (inevitably) the experience of the people you are serving worsens. Look for the most basic of tasks that your shift volunteers can manage. Or look for strong individuals to handle complex project work suited to them. But try not to end up in the middle.

Finally, no matter what model of volunteering works for your organization, you need ways to say thank you. Say it personally and regularly when you interact with your volunteers. Recognize and honor them (when appropriate) in newsletters or on social media. And, if you have a fair number of volunteers, consider holding a volunteer appreciation party every year or every other year.

It always pays to say thank you.

Linda's school tours

When looking around at her options for finding someone else to do the school tours, Linda didn't have solid contenders on staff. The bookkeeper was clearly unsuited for the job and the membership coordinator would be pretty good, but she was a little flighty and also—she had another job to do! If Linda added school tours to her plate, it could overwhelm her other duties.

But Linda didn't see a good way to find the resources to hire someone new just for tours.

It wasn't her first choice, but Linda finally decided that she could create a model that scheduled volunteers for the tours, with staff as backup. Linda would make sure that no volunteer was ever at the cabin alone, so that if there was ever a problem, she or the membership coordinator were on-site. But otherwise, she thought, the ninety minutes of work for a tour could be managed by the volunteer while she did other work in the office.

But it would be too much for any one volunteer, so she would need a roster, each trained to lead a tour. To find the core group of volunteers, she advertised heavily for a volunteer information night in the newsletter and on social media. She asked board members to do the same. That night, she had fifteen people show up, mostly seniors and a couple board members. She presented three kinds of volunteer opportunities:

- Being on a roster to lead school tours, which was a ninety-minute job and volunteers could sign up for tours if they were available.
- Staffing the front desk for a half-day shift, which she thought would appeal to someone who wouldn't mind volunteering but who would prefer to be in a chair and not leading school kids. (This had the added benefit of freeing some hours from the membership coordinator too and giving her more time to get membership-related tasks done.)
- Special project work around historical research or marketing. These were the two areas where Linda wanted the most help and she said it was a special application process.

Linda distributed a sign-up form and talked to people individually that night. Not everyone signed up. But she did get four people who wanted the front desk job and one person interested in the historical research. But most excitingly for her were the five people who said they were interested in leading school tours. Five was enough that she felt she could build a reasonable roster. Even if some of them fell away, there would be a core group. And she made a note to herself to put out the call at least quarterly for more volunteers. She even had one volunteer, Dennis, who asked if he could lead the tour in period clothing from the pioneer days, which sparked a whole new idea for Linda about how the pioneer cabin could connect with schools and the Smallville community. She started to picture what she could do with a team of volunteers, some in period clothes, some not.

Already she'd finished documenting the tour and she planned to work with the volunteers to standardize it. Her plan was to lead the tour with the volunteers shadowing her and then accompany each of them on two or three school tours until they were comfortable taking over on their own. She and the membership coordinator would serve as backups for times when none of the volunteers could do it or if someone fell sick.

Leading the tours in the fall wouldn't be any less work, not at first. But eventually she'd be able to let most of them go, and only do a handful of tours instead of, well, all of them. She hoped it would be just enough to keep connected to the kids.

The prospect of having those hours back for other work was a deep relief to Linda. She hadn't realized how much the tours had come to dominate her fall and spring schedule. But now she wondered what new things she'd be able to do with the time that was now available.

A final note on people

This chapter on people really dominates the first part of the book, but it makes sense—there are so many different things to think about and work on when it comes to people. I've focused on common dynamics in small nonprofits and walking a manager through some first-time experiences like hiring and firing.

If you are still struggling in this area, consider doing some additional reading on managing staff. Classics include *Who Moved My Cheese?* and *The One Minute Manager.*

Even with a book, managing employees can be hard if you've never had to do it before. Again, look for another ED (or a few!) of a similar-sized organization who has been on the job for a while. Ask about some of these questions and listen carefully. Between me and other peers in your community, you should find a path forward for almost any situation.

Onward!

FOUR

THE MONEY

IF YOU COME up with a new idea for a program or a service, at some point you're going to have to ask yourself, "How do we pay for this?" Money is the big question lurking behind both the previous chapters. Whether you are focused on expanding programs or training up your staff, at some point you have to think about the money. How do you spend it? And (perhaps most importantly) how do you get it?

That's what this chapter is about.

Linda's new project for volunteers

As she worked on her volunteer-led tour program, Linda saw new opportunities to grow in ways that the Historical Society had never done before. Costumed volunteers could go to schools and share information. Maybe she could create entire festivals or events with volunteers in period dress. But how to find the revenue to do it? In theory, the volunteers were free, but as she tried to figure out how to make it work, all she saw were the expenses. Working with kids required background checks and paperwork. Events required a whole lot of money. And all these volunteers needed to be trained and managed—who would do that?

Linda herself was the most probable candidate. But having just turned over the school tours to volunteers, she didn't want to have the time she was now saving get filled by volunteer management. There were many other things she would prefer to do.

Linda started to wonder if she could find funding for a part-time volunteer coordinator. Someone in that position could really elevate the entire organization. But where was Linda going to find the resources to make her new idea happen?

Let's talk about money and resources at small nonprofits and help Linda answer her questions.

Nonprofit revenue sources

When it comes to bringing money in the door, nonprofit leaders can often be too focused on current revenue options without considering whether there are new sources of revenue to build up. Building a new source of revenue into something meaningful can take a couple years or more. But making it a priority to improve your finances by diversifying where you get your revenue can build new ways to serve your community.

I want to review some of the most common revenue sources for nonprofits. As you read through these revenue sources, think about how many of them could be new avenues for you to explore.

Federal, state, and city contracts

Governments can't usually "give" money away, but they can contract for services. These are time-consuming grants and can be difficult to get. But once you get them, they can provide a useful base of operational support.

Contracts from the federal government are frequently for "basic needs" like housing. They can run for years and may bring you several hundred thousand or even millions of dollars. But they aren't just given out like candy. The applications are so thick you can measure them in inches and they usually take trained professionals to write. You can't just waltz in and get the money. And the reporting and restrictions on the money are *intense*.

For what it's worth, I've been a team member on a successful lobbying trip to DC, wearing my hat as an elected commissioner on the Metro Parks Board of Tacoma. The team included a school board member, city council member, parks board member (that's me), and several staff members, plus our paid lobbyists. We met with senators and representatives, as well as people in several departments of the federal government. We successfully identified a path to funding from the Department of Commerce, applied, and used those funds to help build a community center. In other words—it took a huge investment of time and resources to learn about the opportunity and then get elected officials on our side. And that was just before the application.

State contracts or grants are similar to federal contracts but everything is at a slightly smaller scale. Less time, less money, less work (depending on your state). I will note that your state elected officials may be more likely than a congressperson to be able to get you some funding. You're more likely to get an appointment and to actually connect with them person-to-person to make something happen. Again, I've been on these lobbying trips. States work differently than the federal government, and a compelling case to the right elected official might really help. It's plenty of work, but the scale is more manageable than what it takes at the federal level (and again, the funding is also probably at a lesser scale too—but for a small nonprofit, that might be just fine).

Finally, we should talk about local funding from your county or city. There are likely a few mechanisms to apply for a variety of different kinds of funding in your community—your nonprofit could get contracts or grants for a wealth of service delivery options depending on what is important in your community right now. These often come from the bureaucracy of the city or county itself. Some of these you might have to apply for and some might come to you because you are really good at what you do and they think you can do the job better than they can.

At the same time, relationships with local elected officials are also a solid option. They might be able to expand a pot of money that funds nonprofits like yours, making it easier for you to apply and secure funds. They might even be able to "put in a good word for you." They might be great sources of information and connect you with the right person or program within city or county government. Or they might even be able to vote on something that funds you directly if they think it's important.

Foundation and private grants

This funding comes from a community foundation or other kind of grant-making foundation. Foundations usually have some sort of application process. Some might ask you to write a full application and submit it. Some might ask you to write a shorter application first, get beyond that hurdle, and then write a longer and more complete application if you're accepted.

(One thing I will note is that there is a slightly squiggly line between a "grant" and a regular "donation." For the purposes of this breakdown, I'm defining a grant as something that comes from an organization, not an individual or a couple.)

Also, something you should know is that foundations often change how they do this process! I spent six years as a volunteer on the distribution committee for the Greater Tacoma Community Foundation, helping to give away several hundred thousand dollars to nonprofits every year. And I can tell you—from the inside, so to speak—that the things we used to evaluate nonprofits and grants were in a constant state of flux. About every two years we had a different way we were supposed to look at the nonprofits. This isn't a bad thing necessarily. The foundation was constantly trying to improve and serve the community, and as the needs changed, so did the grants. But it means that even if you receive a grant from a foundation, you should never take it for granted that it will come again! Sometimes a grant is a trial balloon to see how you do and how you use their funds. Other times, the granting organization might just feel that they want to change how they distribute the funding. One time they will invest deeply with a few nonprofits and another time they will spread the same amount of money more widely. At the end of the day, *people* are making these decisions, and they can be just as capricious and irrational as anyone else, no matter how many supposedly objective ranking forms and checklists they use.

Grants from foundations may go toward specific programs you offer or simply "operational support." The focus of a foundation may also be not just a certain kind of nonprofit, but they might have a certain way they go about making change. For example, several foundations might make grants around homelessness, but within that, some will fund organizations that help with short-term needs like food banks and shelters, while others will try to fund long-term solutions that address the root causes.

These private grants usually have an easier application process than government contracts. There is also usually a person you can pick up the phone and call if you have questions. If you are interested in a grant from a foundation that goes toward "organizational capacity building" and you have no idea what that means, it's worth reaching out and chatting more. Don't just guess, ask! You might be a good fit and you might not. Any good grant officer would rather spend a few minutes answering your questions than spend a bunch of time reviewing an application that doesn't have a chance of making it through their criteria. And you will look better as a nonprofit if you aren't chasing dollars but are being thoughtful about the grants you choose to apply for.

If you don't know where to begin with foundations, here's a place to start: find the annual reports of nonprofits like yours and look at their funders. Then start searching online (and keep a spreadsheet of what you find, including future application dates). You'll get a sense of what doors might be open to you with an afternoon of sleuthing.

Donations from individuals

Ask people for money! It's a really powerful kind of fundraising. I have an entire book about this—*The Little Book of Gold: Fundraising for Small (and Very Small) Nonprofits*—because it's so important.

A single donation of a hundred dollars might not be much, but if you had a hundred donations like that, or a thousand of them, you're talking about real money. Also, if you find a hundred people who want to give you a hundred dollars, some of them are going to be able to give twenty dollars a month ($240/year) if you ask them to increase their gift. And a handful of them might want to give $500 or $1,000. This is called a "donor pyramid." You have a big group of donors giving small amounts of money—that's the base of the pyramid. Above them is a smaller pool of donors giving a little more, and then at the top of the pyramid is a handful of people giving a lot.

Many nonprofit leaders want to skip the bottom of the pyramid. "What if we could just get Bill Gates to give us a million dollars?" they dream. But it doesn't work like that. Most of the time you get small donations and—as you build your relationships over time—the people who want to give more will start to self-identify.

Which leads to the other common mistake—never trying to ask your current donors to "move up" the pyramid. Asking small donors to increase their gift will, over time, fill out "the top of the pyramid."

Small nonprofits are often so reticent to do this that they spend way too much energy trying to find new donors that they take their current donors for granted. If you just keep churning through donors you'll never get anywhere new. The real power in nonprofit fundraising comes from focusing on the people you have.

Consider how you can customize your annual appeal letter or ask. If someone gave $100 last year, can they give $10 or $20 a month this year? And of the pool of people already doing that, can you treat them as your "major" donors and make a personal ask for an even bigger gift? When you ask a donor to "move up" the pyramid, on average one-third to one-fifth of the donors will do it. That success rate is enough to fuel real growth, much faster than searching for new donors every year. It's always easier to build your current base of donors up than it is to find new donors. So put your focus on increasing the donations from current donors more than prospecting for new ones.

Of course, you still want *some* new donors. And what's a good way to get them? Here's one solid answer: events.

Events

There's a whole chapter of *The Little Book of Gold* called "Events Will Kill You." Maybe that's a little hyperbolic, but the fact remains that events are hard work. They are primarily useful for two reasons: getting new donors in the door and creating an easy way to ask your existing donors to give again.

This is one of those areas where small nonprofits can get it really wrong. In this case in particular, it's usually not worth your time to try to follow what the big nonprofits are doing— don't throw a massive gala if you've never done it before. They can make hundreds of thousands—if not millions—of dollars for large nonprofits. But if you haven't seen the events from the inside, you don't see the literally thousands of hours that go into making these events work.

Some small nonprofits can pull them off. Schools can sometimes do it effectively because the volunteer pool can be so big. Parents who want to support their kids can fill all the slots for this—not just the donors for the event, but they are also the volunteers who run it. And the same people who donate items to the auction are also bidding on other items at the event! It's a workable system for schools. I've even seen a day care pull this off because the dynamics are the same. Otherwise, again, proceed cautiously.

My favorite fundraising event for small nonprofits is simple: the fundraising breakfast. It has low cost (no alcohol to pay for and eggs are cheap), low pressure, and yet can still be profitable. It takes plenty of work, and you will need your board to fill tables. But events like this can bring new people into the fold very effectively and also provide a reason for current donors to make another gift. Again, there's a whole chapter about how to create this effectively in *The Little Book of Gold* if this sounds right for your nonprofit.

Planned giving

This is a subset of gifts from individuals, but basically what we're talking about is someone legally locking up a portion of their wealth for you. The most common means of this is including your nonprofit in their estate plan when they pass. For example: "Ten percent goes to the Smallville Historical Society" or "Fifty thousand dollars goes to the Historical Society."

There are other *much* more complicated kinds of planned gifts that are set up by financial planners. Things like charitable gift annuities—the wealth is transferred to your nonprofit and then the donor collects a regular payment from the interest until they pass, at which point you get the interest. All of these take financial planners to set up and are usually only used by people who have real wealth. If you haven't done the steps above to fill out the top of your pyramid, you probably won't have one of these donors drop into your lap. So focus on building a wide donor base and then increasing gifts as you build the pyramid. The more you do that, the more you will find opportunities to attract folks who can plan a gift in this way.

An endowment

The holy grail for nonprofits is a big endowment, where you support your annual budget with the interest earned from your endowment.

If you don't know how it works, imagine that a donor leaves you one million dollars for an endowment. You can't touch the million bucks. But every year, the nonprofit gets roughly three to five percent siphoned off the interest from the principal, depending on how the stock market is doing. Usually it's averaged in some way so that you don't have big ups and downs, so call it *roughly* four percent. That's $40,000 to your nonprofit every year. Forever.

This is pretty great if you have a million dollars in your endowment. But many organizations create an endowment much too early. Having $100,000 in an endowment only earns you $4,000 a year. Most small nonprofits would rather have the $100,000 to spend. So be cautious about locking up funds in an endowment unless you have good reason to think you can increase it quickly. But if you can build it to something real, it can support your nonprofit year after year after year.

Memberships

Most membership-based organizations treat memberships as a blend of fundraising and earned revenue, which is why I'm placing it here between the fundraising that we just talked about and the earned revenue that we'll talk about next. The reason that memberships are a little of both is because they almost always have some sort of tangible benefit to the member, but at the same time, most people actually buy them to support the organization.

The real question, to my mind, is how you pitch it. I often advise "know when you are asking and know when you are selling." By which I mean, sometimes you sell your services ("Come to our musical because it's going to be an amazing night out for the whole family!") and sometimes you ask for support ("Community theater is a vital need and your support will keep it open and accessible for everyone."). Those are distinct strategies.

In general, I think you should *sell* your membership program. Yes, many people will join as a member because they want to support you. But by positioning membership as a way to get discounted or prepaid services, you are making it easier to justify *asking* for donations later.

Earned revenue

Arts nonprofits know a lot about selling tickets, concessions, or merchandise. But many other nonprofits don't consider opportunities for earned revenue.

Is there a way to serve the mission while also improving your bottom line? Sometimes there is!

The example I remember from Peter C. Brinckerhoff's *Mission-Based Management* is to consider a nonprofit that provides services for people with developmental disabilities. This nonprofit almost certainly receives significant grants and government contracts. But could they also create a small business arm that employs the people they serve as cleaners or landscapers? Think of that—a business that provides earned income while also serving the mission!

From my own hometown, I think of the Greek church that throws an annual festival of Greek culture. Food, dancing, and music create a joyful weekend. And they *rake* in the money by selling admission tickets to get in, as well as the food and souvenirs. It's incredibly profitable and—again—not a bad way to introduce people to their culture.

There are other ways to create earned income opportunities without adding a small business or undertaking a major festival.

For example, if your nonprofit currently offers some free services, it might be worth thinking strategically about whether some of these services would be better as paid services that include a sliding scale based on income or an easy way to get a scholarship.

There are a lot of benefits to fees in this case besides the revenue. Even small fees can create incentives for people to show up and do the work because they don't want to "waste money," a dynamic that isn't in play for things that are free. So, in some cases, asking to get paid for some services is actually helpful to the person paying because it makes them more likely to use the service!

Sponsorships are another kind of earned revenue. A sponsorship is a way for a business to market themselves to your audience. If you are a beloved nonprofit, it's good branding for them to position themselves next to you. Usually, it's most appealing to a business if you have a lot of people you can reach.

Functionally, sponsorships are very much like donations. If it helps to frame the difference between a donation and a sponsorship, think of a sponsorship as coming from the marketing budget of a business, while a donation comes from the business owner's pocket. A sponsorship usually involves an agreement about how you will recognize the sponsor—and there might be some negotiations over that part. Once it's secured, it's added revenue for you without having to do too much differently. Again, the key to making this work is having a lot of people you can reach through your marketing or at a central location.

Here's another option for income: teaching. Are you (institutionally speaking) really good at something? Nonprofits may also find earned revenue streams by teaching others what they do. This could be with something formal like an annual conference for people in your field. Or it could be looser—such as quarterly classes or convening a roundtable conversation. Either way, teaching others how to do what you do can help add some earned revenue.

And finally, nonprofits that own their own space may also find revenue renting out portions to other nonprofits. You can look for other nonprofits or even businesses that complement your services.

Some of these revenue ideas carry certain tax implications depending on how close to the mission they are. But they can all help build a more sustainable nonprofit.

Putting it all together

So how does this all work together?

If you are like many nonprofits, one of these areas is your sweet spot. Maybe you're good at earned revenue, maybe you have a team of fundraising volunteers who plan amazing galas, maybe you excel at landing and then managing government contracts. No answer is right, no answer is wrong.

The important point is that I'd like you to look for a *mix*.

If you are too reliant on one single form of revenue, you open yourself to risk, it's as simple as that. The nonprofit that gets most of its revenue from selling tickets...is at risk during extended quarantines due to pandemics (also a risk for the organization that gets their revenue from big fundraising galas). Government contracts are at risk during recessions. Foundation grants and individual donations may be at risk if you are having a public relations crisis.

So the goal is to think about building new streams of income that mix up your total revenue. This isn't just as simple as adding different kinds of revenue. When I was at the Grand Cinema, most of our revenue came from movie ticket sales. I intensely studied the business of the Grand and significantly improved concessions revenue. And while that was nice to have, it was still reliant on the same thing—people coming into the theater to see movies. So the additional educational programs, grant writing, membership, and individual fundraising I worked to build was probably more important to the organization because it wasn't reliant on the same thing.

Again, more revenue is good, but seeking a balance of different kinds of revenue is even better.

The other benefit of different revenue sources is cash flow, something I'll talk about a lot more below. Government contracts can have very long periods of time between payments. Fundraising events can eat up your money for months before you hope to earn it all back and then some. Earned revenue might require an investment in staff or merchandise before you can see any benefit. Depending on how these interact with each other, there might be periods of weeks or even months when you are barely able to make payroll. As you look for new sources of revenue, keep an eye out for sources that can provide cash flow during slow times.

Is there a "right" amount for balancing different kinds of revenue sources?

I can't give a single answer that will be accurate for all the many different kinds of nonprofits out there. But I can safely say this: If you have more than ninety percent of your revenue come from the same place, you're opening yourself up to possible problems. If something goes wrong, what then?

Here's a good goal, regardless of where you are right now: whatever your secondary or tertiary sources of revenue are...can you double them over the next couple of years? So, if you get ninety-five percent of your revenue from the same place, can you build your other sources of revenue to become ten percent instead of five percent? If you get twenty percent of your revenue from secondary sources, can you build those revenue sources to forty percent?

It might be hard. But over time, it will pay off.

The more you can balance your revenue, the stronger you will be.

When all your eggs are in one basket...

That said, if all your eggs are truly in one basket, then watch that basket! Monitor it carefully through a dashboard of important metrics and set regular reminders to yourself to look at some ways to keep your performance up. Don't take it for granted and work to earn that revenue every day and every year.

Let's talk about budgets

Now that you have a sense of where you can make your revenue and how you might split it up, we need to get into the nitty-gritty details of money. And our best tool is going to be a budget.

Many very small nonprofits try to get away with operating without a budget. This is almost always the wrong approach for most nonprofits, especially those with dreams of growing.

You need a budget!

Let me give you an example of a common scenario at an organization that doesn't have a budget. The Executive Director wants to sign a contract with an outside graphic designer to design a new logo. It's going to be $500, which is above the threshold she can sign herself. So she brings the proposed contract to the board president who is wary of signing on his own. He says it should go to the board for approval. One board member wants to review the bids she got from other designers. One board member wants to review the work samples of the selected designer. Another board member questions whether they can really afford this right now. Is it the best use of $500?

A half hour (or more!) passes and eventually the board takes a vote on whether to approve the expense.

Here's the deal: it doesn't even matter whether the board voted to go ahead with the contract or not because, either way, the process was a waste of everyone's time and energy. It's also —and I feel strongly about this if you can't tell already—an abdication of the Executive Director's role to manage operations.

Here's how a budget can help. Instead of arguing about each individual expenditure, you can plan ahead and estimate things in advance. What do you think your fundraiser will cost to produce? What do you think you'll spend on Facebook ads? What do you think you will spend on office supplies? Sometimes you can use last year's expenditures to get a good range, sometimes you can plan for a certain number, and sometimes you just guess. The point is, the ED puts together a budget, proposes it to the board, and gets everything approved *all at once*.

So there's a real time savings a budget can bring you. Yes, the budget process itself can be a lot of work. But overall, it usually works out to be a better use of time than continued expenditure approvals month after month.

Using the budget to go over finances also keeps the roles clearer for the board and the Executive Director too. Think about the budget as a board policy expressed in numbers. They are telling the Executive Director "this is how we want you to manage the nonprofit." So it's a board policy, and by keeping them at that level they aren't getting into the operations of the nonprofit.

Ideally, this budget should be created by the Executive Director and presented to the board to review and eventually approve. There's real power when you—the person who will be in charge of implementing the budget—take the lead in actually creating it. No one else knows the ins and outs of the budget as well as the ED. It's hard to manage a budget you didn't create. So if you take the lead on this, you can both keep the board out of your hair on the daily operations as well as create a budget you feel confident in—because you helped to create it!

I like starting the budget process three to four months before the end of the fiscal year. So if your fiscal year follows the calendar year, here's a sample timeline:

- The Executive Director starts modeling a new budget in September, only seen by herself at this point.
- When she has something she's relatively happy with, she presents the budget to the finance committee in October (or the executive committee or just the treasurer if you don't have a finance committee).
- The ED makes tweaks based off of that feedback and presents the next draft to the full board in November, possibly with one more stop at the finance committee along the way. This is the main topic of that board meeting.
- In December, the ED makes tweaks based on the feedback from the November board meeting and brings the budget back for final approval. This should be fairly routine and take only a few minutes. The tone for the ED is: "Here's a rundown of the changes I made based on your feedback last month and here's how the final numbers shook out. We'd like your approval so we can implement it next month." Easy.

That process is a reasonable timeframe that balances all the roles pretty well. Executive Directors shouldn't wait and hope for something like this to happen either. Take the initiative and start planning ahead.

Finally, budgets are worth the time for one big reason that I haven't touched on—they give you goals! They force you to consider questions of revenue and expenses months before they actually happen. This exercise is hugely helpful.

Story time: I once consulted with a rapidly growing nonprofit that was, nevertheless, stuck. There were real growing pains and both the founder (who was serving as board president) and the Executive Director were stymied. I worked with both of them individually and I worked with the full board. But one of the most important things I did was sit down with the Executive Director to create an annual budget.

The organization had never had one and the first-time ED wasn't sure it was worth the time or how to even construct one. I spent an hour to ninety minutes going through budgeting with her, filling in income and expenses on a blank budget template. I asked lots of questions. What if you hired a new employee in September? How much did you make during the last two auctions, and what are your goals for this next year? We covered it all and put them in the budget.

When we were done, we had mapped out the next year of finances for the nonprofit—and the nonprofit looked incredibly strong and financially healthy. The fears were unfounded. But it took building a budget to see that.

How to write a budget

I want to start this by reminding you that I have a template available at http://bit.ly/LBONLbonuses if you want a sample twelve-month budget to use. So I'm not going to linger too long on the technicalities of creating the spreadsheet, since that tool is available to you!

But a blank spreadsheet isn't necessarily enough to write your own, so here are some useful tips for actually creating a budget.

Twelve-month budgets help you visualize the year.

I really like a budget that gives you space to plan for each month, not just the total year. My sample budget for small nonprofits fits on a single page, but it still includes twelve columns for each month.

This kind of budgeting helps you understand how money will come in and out over the course of the year. One reason this is useful is that you can see if there are any long periods where you think the nonprofit will lose money. It's good to catch this in advance (and we'll talk more about it shortly when we talk about cash flow).

A twelve-month budget is also useful if you want to consider making changes partway through the year. What if you want to add a new employee in September—how will having that employee change your expense line for the last four months of the year? It's much easier (and clearer for a board member to understand) if you adjust expenses for those four months instead of lumping it all together as a single staff line item in an annual budget.

If you finish your budget work and discover that you're "in the hole," it's usually easier to find more realistic cost savings or new revenue ideas if you're looking at a twelve-month budget than if you're looking at a single column for the entire year.

Use historical data to make an informed budget.

Choosing the right number to put into a budget line can be

tricky. It's part art and part science. I'll give you an example from the Smallville Historical Society.

For the last three years, the Smallville Historical Society has made $10,000, $12,000, and $15,000 through their membership program. How much should Linda budget for next year?

Here are her options:

- She could budget for an average of the last three years—$12,333
- She could budget for what she made the year before —$15,000
- She could budget based on the rising pattern of memberships—in this case somewhere between $16,000 or $18,000
- She could budget for a stretch goal—which could be $20,000 or even more

Is there a right answer for what Linda should budget for membership next year? Well, as is often the case, the answer is: it depends.

Most of the time, budgeting for an average of the last few years or budgeting for whatever you made (or spent) the year before is pretty safe. Projecting for small increases can also be easily justified.

Stretch goals are tricky. On the one hand, if you keep budgeting for no revenue growth you will probably have...no revenue growth. Budgeting for growth can actually help you achieve growth! But the more a budget becomes an aspirational document, the less useful it is as a financial one.

My recommendation is that you budget for either no growth or small growth in most revenue categories and then choose a single area of focus for a stretch goal. So you might budget modestly in memberships, grants, earned revenue, and your annual appeal, while budgeting for a stretch goal in what you hope to get back from major gift requests (for example). But whatever you choose to make a stretch goal, now is the time to plan for what you actually do to achieve it!

Budget for a fraction of the grants you need.

Here's another handy tip—don't budget to win every grant you apply for! Therein lies disaster. Many organizations budget to receive only a third (or maybe even a quarter) of the grants they apply for. Some nonprofits might have relationships with funders that make them more confident about the likelihood of certain grants. In those cases you can feel better about budgeting the full amount, or budgeting for a half or three-quarters of the expected grant, to reflect that there is always some level of uncertainty.

The goal is that losing a single grant shouldn't blow a massive hole in your program budget. If you have multiple options and are planning to only get a few of them, you're much more likely to make this happen.

Should you budget to "make money?"

Many nonprofit leaders are wary of budgeting for "profit." The thinking goes, "We're a nonprofit, so doesn't that mean we should have no profits?"

I'm here to emphatically say that this is not true. It is ok to end the year with some extra money—in fact, it's a good thing! We'll talk about reserves next, but here's how you can handle this situation at your nonprofit.

If you finish your budget work and you see there's some extra money, you can add a line to your budget and designate it to reserves. This gives you a "zero budget" which means you're not showing a profit anymore on the budget. If anyone on your board is in the "no profits" camp, this will almost always appease them.

The flip side of this is also true. If you think you will end the year down a bit (or a lot) you can show an amount coming from reserves to cover it—assuming the money is there. Most of the time, you should not budget to lose money. Let's say you have a healthy amount of cash reserves and you are using a portion of it to fund a new strategic initiative—that might be a good reason to lose some money. I can't think of many more. Don't get complacent about losing money. But if you do need to budget for a loss for some reason, this is a good way to present it.

Linda's funding for her new program

Linda was trying to figure out how to create more programs in the community to leverage the historical reenactors who were suddenly very excited about volunteering for the Historical Society. There were costs to everything, but the biggest cost was that she strongly felt like she needed a part-time volunteer coordinator to help manage them, as she didn't want either of her current staff members doing it. She estimated what a part-time volunteer coordinator would cost the nonprofit (using the tools in the previous chapter to establish a salary range).

Once she had the number, she went about figuring out how to pay for that position.

There were two "organizational capacity" grants that she thought she could apply for—this seemed like the kind of project they would support for the first year, maybe two, to help get it off the ground. She budgeted to receive only one of them.

She also thought that this new program would look really good in an annual appeal. The photos of costumed volunteers with kids might really tug at heartstrings, and she thought she could find some donors who would support it as well. There were also new potential donors she would reach, which could help fundraising too. She projected a modest increase there as well. And for the first year, she would do a special callout for this program at the annual fundraiser, which would hopefully help get it off the ground as well.

She didn't want to ask for any earned revenue from the schools if she could avoid it—she thought it would turn off schools from bringing the Historical Society in. But she thought that she could structure the off-site educational visits to help with marketing the cabin. What if the volunteers passed out 2-for-1 coupons? Or a "kids come free" coupon? That might boost the number of people coming to the cabin, which increased not only ticket sales but also merchandise sales. She budgeted a small increase there as well.

And there were small grants from the school district and city to fund some after-school programs. It was a stretch, but maybe she could find something there. She didn't budget for anything from it yet, but she knew she would try to get some of that funding as well.

Putting all those sources together, it was enough for her to feel reasonably confident that—if she got at least one of the two capacity grants—she could start the hiring process for a part-time volunteer coordinator.

Now that she knew that's where her focus needed to be, she put as much work as she could into those two applications. As soon as she got a yes from either one of them, she was ready to move forward.

Excel

As we start really working with numbers, this is a good time to say that I very strongly advocate getting friendly with Microsoft

Excel or Google Sheets. Look at how Linda planned for a possible new volunteer coordinator. It's hard to do without a spreadsheet.

What if you want to build revenue by changing your membership model? The model will raise the membership price by twenty percent but because of the higher prices, you expect at least ten percent not to renew. Is this plan a good idea or a bad idea? A calculator can help you figure that out if you can keep track of the figures. But Excel takes it to the next level. For that twenty percent membership increase, Excel can help you model three variants—twenty percent loss of members (poor), ten percent loss of members (fair), no loss of members (great)—and then you will have numbers to make you feel better about a course of action.

Not everyone is at home with Excel, which I get. But *please* don't throw up your hands and assume that it always has to be the case. You can absolutely improve your skills. There are many Excel tutorials out there, most of them free. This will help your work as an Executive Director immensely.

Understanding cash flow

I've used the term "cash flow" and I want to make sure we've got a clear definition here. Basically it's a way to evaluate whether you have money in the bank to pay your bills. You have "positive cash flow" if you are making more money than you spend and you have "negative cash flow" if you are spending more than you make. But cash flow is mostly important as we project *forward*.

Here's a great example of a cash flow question—the Smallville Historical Society just finished their annual fundraiser and Linda doesn't expect any new income until she gets money from the state contract in another three months. *Does she have enough money in the bank to make it until then?*

How would she go about figuring out the answer to that question?

Back-of-the-envelope cash flow

Linda can answer this math problem by looking at how much she has in the bank *right now*. Not what the statement says, but what is actually in her account at this very moment. Anything that's actual cash, she counts. That's the first piece of data she needs. Then, she takes her annual budget for expenses and divides by twelve. That will give her a monthly average of expenses. That's the second piece of data she needs. Now she compares these numbers. If she has $45,000 in the bank, and—on average—the nonprofit spends $15,000 a month, then she has "three months" of reserves, which means she should be able to get to the next big payment.

But only just. What if the state pays late? What if the next three months have slightly higher than normal expenses?

This is where the back-of-the-envelope method breaks down. If a nonprofit has plenty of money, and this method always shows four, five, or six months of money in the bank, then more detailed cash flow work isn't necessary. But for all of us who aren't so lucky...we need more detail.

Really crunching the numbers for cash flow

Good news! I have a sample cash flow report template that I use regularly, plus a video where I walk through the creation of a full nonprofit cash flow report using real world numbers. Like the rest of the bonuses in the book, you can find the link at http://bit.ly/LBONLbonuses. It's a useful way to understand how to model your own nonprofit's cash flow because you will actually see me working with a spreadsheet. I highly recommend it.

Almost no nonprofit has finances that are as simple as the above example. Usually there's a mix of money coming in over time, and the money going out can be highly seasonal. So actually estimating when you will get paid for certain things, and when you will make payments for others, is crucial.

Once, I created a cash flow report and discovered that I needed to lay off an employee. It was not a good feeling. But do you know what a worse feeling would be? Finding out that I needed to lay her off *too late*.

I've also used cash flow reports to plan for investments of new technology or other big expenditures. Wherever the numbers take you, going through the steps is vital to leading your organization and not falling into financial pits that you could have avoided with a little bit of foresight and an Excel spreadsheet.

Here's what you'll need to run the numbers:

- An hour or so of quiet time in front of a computer.
- A budget, if you have one (and hopefully you do!).
- The last two months of bank statements (use the copies that came in the mail, or print the PDFs from the bank. It's easier than flipping back and forth between screens).

Again, the specific steps to creating this document are all on my website at http://bit.ly/LBONLbonuses.

My recommendations for an Executive Director is that you should know the state of cash flow at any given point in the year. I *don't* mean you need to run these reports every day. I mean that once you run it, you should keep that information in mind as you're making your decisions.

If it shows that money is extraordinarily tight, then run it monthly—or even more frequently—and hold off on inessential purchases. If the report shows that you are doing great for the next several months, then you can run the report quarterly and rest easy knowing that a sudden unexpected expense won't be fatal.

Budgets and cash flow

Getting a solid budget for your organization and an understanding of your nonprofit's cash flow position are the two most important things you can do to understand and then manage the finances of your nonprofit. Yes, finding new revenue is important too. But no matter how much revenue, you still need a budget. You still need to understand cash flow. Do these two things and you'll find that revenue starts increasing as well.

I want to end this chapter on money with a few principles that should help you evaluate your own nonprofit's revenue and spending.

Some small expenses can save you thousands

Most nonprofits spend a majority of their income on *people*. We've talked a lot about people earlier, but it's worth reiterating here your biggest expense will almost certainly be staffing costs. How you divvy that up will depend on everything we just covered in this chapter and the previous one.

Good people on staff are your biggest assets too, as we've talked about. They are ambassadors to donors—a good interaction with a happy staff member at the front desk can turn someone into a major donor. They know the work—a good program manager can live your mission in a way that builds confidence in your program and leads to new grants. Good people are important.

And yet, nonprofit managers often deny their staff basic tools because they are reluctant to spend money on anything *but* people.

I listened to a story recently of a low-wage employee who spent hours and hours of her week messing around with PDF reports and extracting the information out of them. She asked her boss for a piece of software that would enable her to do the work in a matter of minutes instead of hours. It was a couple hundred dollars. And she was denied the software because it was too expensive. She eventually left because she was unhappy—and part of it was feeling like her day-to-day experience of her job wasn't very fulfilling anymore.

But regardless of whether she stayed or she left, her boss made a terrible financial choice by denying the software purchase. No matter what this person was paid, spending hours and hours on something every week that could be done in *minutes* is a bad use of money. They paid her thousands of dollars to do the work without the software. Spending a couple hundred on the software was a *savings*.

Nonprofit managers make this mistake all the time, because they don't see the cost of staff. Or, put another way, they see staff costs as being flat. Whether her boss bought the software or not, her pay wouldn't change. So it can be easy to think that that staff cost isn't "real" somehow when making this kind of calculation.

These managers don't see the ongoing cost of having someone do inefficient work that could be solved with a piece of relatively cheap software or even with something as simple as a changed workflow. Or they don't put money into professional development because it's expensive. But if you have a good employee, giving her additional training to do her job better is a *fantastic* use of money. It's a far better use of money than losing that employee, finding someone else, and having to train them up.

Of course, all of these lessons can be taken to extremes, so don't overlearn this part. An in-state conference is much cheaper for the nonprofit than one across the country, or in another country. A $200 piece of software is different than buying all new laptops for everyone because the ones you have are a little old and a little slow. The magnitude is totally different. But *small* expenses such as these really pay off *when they are focused on the employee.*

Resilience versus efficiency

Sometimes it's hard to see the water we swim in and realize there might be another way. One of the places this is most clear to me is how far the goal of "efficiency" has permeated the world's business culture. It's so a part of our assumptions that we often see efficiency as a good in and of itself, and to question it is—by its nature—inefficient. And isn't inefficiency inherently bad?

It's *not.* The opposite of efficiency isn't always inefficiency. Sometimes the opposite is *resilience.* When I advocate for things like cross-training between employees, professional development, or getting three months of expenses into reserves, you are making your organization slightly more inefficient. And that's ok! You are making it dramatically more resilient too. Because when something goes wrong—whether it's as large as a pandemic or as small as an employee leaving suddenly—you will appreciate having invested the energy in striving for resiliency.

As always, there's a balance. But don't automatically assume that efficiency is the only worthy goal. Resilience might cost you a little more in the short term, whether in time or money, but it will pay off.

Pricing and cost recovery

After twelve years on the board of Metro Parks Tacoma, I learned a lot about how a government agency thinks about service delivery and revenue collection.

Metro Parks has some services that are a public good and some services that are highly individualized. Parks are open to everyone. Little League teams have a big public benefit but also aren't for everyone (people without kids don't benefit directly, but they do in some secondary ways). And the benefits of private adult kayaking lessons are very much to the individual kayaker—no one else but the kayaker can plausibly benefit from these lessons.

So how did Metro Parks price them? They structured their pricing and cost recovery to mirror the level of community benefit. Things with wide community benefit had low cost recovery. Parks are free and paid for entirely by taxes. Little League fees are small and kept very low, with a portion of the cost of the program subsidized by other money. But things like private adult kayaking lessons were priced to *make* money. Things like that needed to be profitable, so that those things would support the other community-minded programs and services.

Your nonprofit may not have the same kind of dynamic as a government agency but I encourage you to look at your programs and services with this lens. Are your highly individualized services priced to generate profit? Could those create a new source of revenue that would support your community-wide services so that you could reduce the price?

Which brings us to our next topic!

Thinking about what is fundable and what is not

Some programs appeal to grant support from foundations, others to individual donors, and others won't appeal to any donor—you'd be better to find earned revenue or just any general unrestricted donation to support those.

One of the skills you'll hone over the years as an Executive Director is figuring out how to fund your programs. Some of this will come from your experience with individual donors—the more you know your donors, the more you will know what they care about. Then, when an idea crosses your desk that matches it, you'll know exactly where to take it. You'll also gain experience from following your regular funders. What buzzwords are they using when they solicit grants? Who are they funding and how is it changing? Keep an eye on these.

And sometimes you may see funding potential simply because an idea, for lack of a better word...sizzles. People respond to new and interesting ideas. Or maybe there's something you're already doing but there's an idea that makes it feel new again—a little topspin that grabs attention. If you can imagine something as a feel-good story on the nightly news, that might be a good sign that a donor or foundation would be interested as well.

———

Mission, people, money

This ends the first section of the book that divides attention among three areas—mission, people, money. They are all absolutely intertwined and an Executive Director will not be able to successfully manage a nonprofit without having a handle on all three areas.

But it's not enough to just manage a nonprofit! Your job title is not Executive Manager. We need to lead. But what does that mean when we're also an employee of a board of directors? We'll investigate the ED/board relationship in the next section.

PART TWO

WORKING FOR A BOARD OF DIRECTORS

FIVE

TEN COMMANDMENTS FOR WORKING WITH BOARDS

I SAID this in the first chapter, but it's important to come back to: working for a board is a highly unusual professional working relationship. No single person can tell you what to do, and yet collectively they can fire you. They don't get paid for their work, but you do. They come and go, but you stay.

It's *odd*.

And it can be hard.

But it can also be pretty great.

I've had full-time nine-to-five salaried jobs, I've been self-employed, and I've been a nonprofit Executive Director. Being a nonprofit ED is a great blend of the best parts of a salaried job and the best parts of being self-employed. You have the steady income that comes with a salaried job. And you also have some of the flexibility that comes with being self-employed. As daily work environments go, it's hard to beat.

The key is to do the work, to make sure the board knows you're doing the work, and to help them do *their* work. Here are ten things you should know that will really help you do that.

1. Let the board govern itself

Sometimes it can be tempting to meddle in board business, but except in the more dire of situations, you should endeavor to stay out of it. Let's say Linda doesn't particularly like one of the people who wants to be board president next year. Maybe she knows (or suspects) they are difficult or have their own agenda or whatever it is. She might be tempted to say something along those lines to some of the other board members to try to sway the vote.

No!

Stay away from this. Even board members who might agree with Linda will likely still be worried about a nonprofit ED who does this. It's the same fear people will have about any gossiper: "If she's saying this about someone else, what is she saying about me?" But in this case, the gossiper works for them.

This is not just true about people but is also true of policies that are about board governance. Let's say an ED sees a need for term limits on the board. On almost every board, this is a fraught, if not controversial, policy discussion. Introducing term limits can scare board members if not handled correctly. One way to handle it poorly is for the ED to tell the board that they really need term limits! This is unlikely to sit well with the board. An ED will almost always do better to focus her energy on creating the space for those policies to arise from the board itself.

That could include lending support to a governance committee, assisting with a review of the bylaws, or otherwise facilitating board members to find resources (like my website, my book on boards, 501commons.org, boardsource.org, or other resources for nonprofit boards) that help them make these decisions on their own. By all means, encourage your leadership to have facilitated retreats or to carve out time for board development. But as to the *specifics* of what they do, don't thrust your own agenda on them. If you exert just a light touch or put "a thumb on the scale," you will get farther than you will trying to manage the board "from below."

Now, having written that, let me offer some small exceptions to this commandment.

I have, on occasion, been in the room when the executive committee is talking about future officers and I have weighed in *when I had something positive to say.* I have also privately suggested to individual board members that they would be great as officers and that I'd love to work more closely with them. I'm talking about positive words in small groups or one-on-one. I think that is appropriate. Venturing into anything more will get you in hot water.

I'm also more open about my ideas in committees. If a controversial proposal like term limits is being discussed in a committee, I will talk about some of the benefits and drawbacks —again, often with a thumb on the scale. But if the full board is in a deep argument about it at a board meeting, I will do my best to sit quietly until I'm invited into the discussion (and there again, I will try to be as reasonable as possible so as not to offend one side or another if there are factions). In this way, I can help guide what gets to the board, but I'm not taking a side in an argument.

There is another place where you can play a role in keeping a board on task and committed—being their "clerk," so to speak. If the board creates a governance committee, but it hasn't met in a few months, go ahead and email the chair and ask when the date of the next meeting is "because you're trying to plan your schedule." If the board has committed to strategic planning, you can remind the president it should be on the agenda. These gentle nudges can add up in a positive way and they shouldn't be considered interference in actual board business.

2. Board members are board members first

I once knew an Executive Director who was really struggling with his board, the board's leadership, and the general direction of the nonprofit. He voiced his frustrations and grievances to a board member, who was also a friend.

After mulling it over for a few days, that board member took those concerns to the leadership of the board. The leadership didn't like being questioned and fired the Executive Director shortly thereafter. The ED was shocked at this turn of events and he took it up with his board member friend. The board member told the Executive Director that he felt bad about betraying a confidence, but he also felt like it was his duty to relay the ED's feelings to the full board. That it was an employment issue and as a board member, he felt obliged to pass it along. He was his friend, yes, but he was also a board member.

This is an extreme example, but it should be clear. It is totally fine to be friends with board members. But if you complain about the board...if you tell that board member friend you're going to resign at the end of the year and haven't shared that news with the rest of the board too...it's possible that it won't just stay between you and the board member. When it comes to the nonprofit, friends on the board are board members first.

Imagine that they are in a club. Anything you confide in a board member, or complain about, has a strong likelihood of getting to the rest of the members of the club. So if you are frustrated or angry or at all upset with your board, don't unload it onto a board member, even if that board member is also your friend.

The one board member you should be able to be open and honest with is the board president. To have realistic conversations about the nonprofit, both the ED and the board president should feel like they can talk about personalities and frustrations. I believe this is an important relationship and you should strive to build the trust needed to make it work. But if, for whatever reason, the trust isn't there to have this kind of conversation openly, then I would strongly recommend that you put a professional face on all the relationships you have with your board members.

3. Never surprise your board president at a meeting

As I just mentioned, I believe that you should do whatever you can to cultivate a good relationship with your board president. Weekly breakfast meetings, regular chats, and more. This relationship is, in many ways, the hinge that the nonprofit relies on. The two of you can disagree, and you can argue in private. But you should try to be on the same page in public. Or at least have mutual understanding.

As part of this, I believe you should do everything you can to avoid surprising the board president at the meeting.

I've done it. Through omission, forgetfulness, or just because I thought I had a problem handled that in retrospect I clearly did not. So I can speak from experience here. Board presidents don't like it, and if you're trying to build that relationship, this is a setback.

Do your best to avoid the situation with regular updates.

4. Assume leadership

You are in charge of the day-to-day operations of the nonprofit. Act like it. If it's within budget, policies, and the strategic plan, it's your decision to make—not the board's.

For the sake of keeping up the momentum of the nonprofit, you're going to have to do what you were hired to do: lead the operations of the nonprofit. Sometimes it might mean that you have to ask for forgiveness, or accept a reprimand. But generally speaking, you need to be willing to step up and do your job. If you keep running every single decision by the board, the nonprofit won't be able to move forward. There will be too many cooks in the kitchen.

Yes, some decisions are delicate enough or political enough that it behooves you to get input from the board or a committee before you go ahead. But in my experience, a board will always weigh in *if you invite them*, so be careful and be specific when you do so.

If this isn't the kind of working relationship you have with the board, then start with small things. These should be obvious and noncontroversial choices. Do them, and then inform the board about what you've done. Keep that up for a while and you'll find it gets easier and easier to do the big things.

5. Submit a written monthly report

At my first board meeting as managing director of the Grand Cinema, I brought a written report of everything I'd done for the month. I swear a board member almost cried. He'd felt so far out of the loop before I was hired that my two pages were that meaningful to him.

It was a good lesson. Write a report!

What did you do this month? Write it down and send it to the board as part of the board packet (which will also include meeting minutes, finances, the agenda, and supporting documents).

I've honed my report style since that first meeting. I write a monthly report that includes three to five big things that I want the board to know (and that I want them to know I worked hard on) and then I include a list of "other tasks and accomplishments" for the month. I keep the report short—one to two pages —and then I cover some highlights or add any updates at the meeting itself. That usually only takes a few minutes.

Remember, board members don't see you day in and day out. Most of what they know of your performance is what they see at board and committee meetings. It's important to keep them in the loop on what you actually do.

I've included a couple sample reports at http://bit.ly/ LBONLbonuses. These are real reports I've used at different nonprofits, so they should give you a good sense of how I've communicated with my board.

6. Attend as many committee meetings as you can

The work of the board should really happen at committee meetings. Attending them and listening is very useful. As the ED, you can keep committees from working at cross-purposes and be an information liaison. You can also accept work assignments.

In fact, I think it's important to "staff" these meetings. Take down tasks and then bring back the results of your work at the next meeting. You should be an essential (but unofficial) member of the committee in that regard. Boards and committees are usually great for decision-making. But they aren't as good at *doing*. You can be the doer.

Another reason to be at these meetings is that, every so often, a committee might meet without you present and start on a path that is not feasible or that you have to walk back somehow. This can create hurt feelings while you try to put the genie back in the bottle. Be the cat herder who keeps everyone (roughly) moving in the same direction.

The final reason to staff committees is that these folks are your bosses! Collectively speaking, at least. If you let the committees meet without you, then you're really only getting face time with your bosses once a month. I think that's too long. Engage with your board and support the committees.

7. When in doubt, refer ideas back to the board's committees

One of the most frustrating challenges to deal with as an Executive Director is when a board member calls you up or emails you with their "suggestions." Even good ideas that come to you this way can be hard to manage, because you may not have the budget or time to implement them. It can be awkward to tell a board member (who happens to make decisions about your employment status) that her idea is not workable. Some board members are fine hearing that, but others may think of you as "their" employee and get disgruntled when you don't take their advice or ideas and implement them immediately.

How best to handle that situation? My recommendation is to always refer these ideas and suggestions back to the board level. For example: "Interesting idea! Why don't you bring this up at the next marketing committee meeting and see what they think?"

This relieves you of needing to be the bad guy who kills a board member's idea.

You can also refer a board member in these situations to the documents that the board itself passed. The board passed a budget. The board passed a strategic plan. The board passed policies. If the idea being pitched is not budgeted for, if it doesn't fit within the strategic plan, or if implementing it would break a policy, it's fine to point that out. For example: "The budget the board gave me to work with won't allow us to implement that this year. But why don't we work with the finance committee to see if we can make it work for the next fiscal calendar?" Or: "It's an intriguing idea. But the strategic plan the board passed says that we should be moving away from a model like what you're suggesting. Maybe the board should look at your idea and weigh it against the current plan at the next retreat."

This puts the burden of follow-up on the board member, which is where it should be. You do work for the board, but each board member is not your direct supervisor, if that distinction makes sense. When a board member approaches you with ideas out of committees or the board meeting, your best bet is to do whatever you can to redirect them back into the board and committee structure and let the board deal with those ideas itself.

As I hope it's clear with these last two commandments, committees are your friend! They relieve the pressure on the board meetings to get work done there, they give good face time for you, and they are a good place to divert board members if they go "rogue" with suggestions and ideas.

8. *Never* fudge the numbers

This might be assumed, but it's worth being one hundred percent clear about. If things are hard for a few months, you might be tempted to portray the numbers in a way that is... misleading. Not even dishonest. Just...misleading.

Do it a few times and you might find yourself sliding from presenting numbers that are misleading to numbers that are outright lies. A treasurer with any financial background will start to smell that the books are being cooked.

I'm not even talking about doing anything illegal, necessarily. At the Grand, we operated under accrual accounting. (That means that some expenses and income are accounted for in different months than the money was paid or received.) The accounting system makes sense, but it meant that my book-keeper and I regularly talked about which month a certain transaction should be placed. Sometimes during "bad" months, I could feel the temptation to answer these questions in ways that would make the month look better than it actually was. But robbing from December to make November look better...just creates an issue in December. The more an ED gets used to this, the easier it will be for her to actually pull a fast one later.

The coverup is far worse than having a loss on the books.

The numbers are the numbers. Present them honestly no matter what they say.

9. Identify possible new board members

In the course of your work, you will run across dedicated volunteers, generous donors, and community leaders who might make ideal candidates for the board. If you work well with someone you meet, or if you see her work well in a group setting, then go ahead and ask her if she would considered standing for nomination. Tell her about the nonprofit and the work you do. If she is interested, refer her to the board during the nominations process. You can certainly make it clear that you don't get to make this decision alone. But you can tell her the process and do an email introduction or otherwise facilitate a "getting to know you" meeting.

You are in a great position to see candidates that the board never would have seen. Refer them on. Just identifying good quality candidates is a solid start to making sure that in the long run, you have quality prospects to fill seats on the board. If you do that often enough, you will build a great board with people you know you can work with.

10. Do the work

Hopefully, you are the ED of a nonprofit because you are committed to the work that they do. Whatever is going on with the board, you need to keep your focus on the work.

This implies a trust in the board...but even more than that it requires that you give up some amount of control to them. (EDs often have trouble here—myself included. But trying to control everything just doesn't work.) Come to meetings prepared, and do your best to support the board in their work. But don't get sucked too far into board politics or drama. Your employees, your volunteers, and your community are expecting you to do good things. Do the work, and trust the board to do theirs.

Bonus! 11. Help your board help themselves

Here's a bonus tip that's also a bit of self-promotion as well. You can download a free preview of *The Little Book of Boards* at http://bit.ly/LBONLbonuses to see if this is the right resource to help your board continue to improve. This is a special preview of the book that I created just for Executive Directors to see the key messages I give boards about their responsibilities and duties to the organization and the board. Please check it out and if you like it, I hope you will consider referring it to your board president. A lot of boards of small nonprofits can use a little help with governance and a resource like this—that is tailored exactly for a small nonprofit board—could be ideal for your organization.

———

Follow these commandments and your relationship with the board will stay on a steady course.

SIX

GETTING THE MOST FROM YOUR BOARD

NOT EVERYONE IS BLESSED with a great board right off the bat. How do you get the most out of your board? And how does an Executive Director—from "below"—help the board grow and flourish (while still respecting the ten commandments in the previous chapter)?

The pendulum of board engagement

Board engagement tends to resemble the path of a pendulum. On the one end of the pendulum's arc, the board is disengaged and barely aware of the day-to-day operations of the nonprofit. On the other end, the board is incredibly active and is micromanaging the work of the Executive Director.

Neither end is good for you, the ED.

Yes, if you have a micromanaging board, it might be *tempting* to wish that the board would be disengaged. "Wouldn't it be great if they would just stay out of my hair and let me do the real work of running the nonprofit?" But any nonprofit ED who has been in this situation will tell you it's not all it's cracked up to be. These EDs don't have board support for fundraising, for bouncing ideas off of, or for, well...anything. In the short run, this means the nonprofit isn't operating to its fullest potential. On any given day, it's probably not an issue that is noticeably hurting the organization. But this situation always runs the risk of blowing up into a crisis. Worse, a disengaged board can make simple problems *into* crises.

How? Well, inevitably, some incident will make the board realize that they should have been paying attention all along, and then they go into freak-out mode and overcompensate. The board will be gathering information on the fly, and they might listen to an outsider as readily as their hired staff.

What they choose to do about the crisis is anyone's guess. The pendulum could swing all the way across the spectrum and the board could be in micromanagement mode for a few months or a year. Or they might make some dramatic change against the ED's wishes. They might even fire the ED, thinking that they are solving the problem with a staff change.

And the ED is unlikely to have much say in what they do because there's no trust between the ED and the board. And how could there be? The board was disengaged and didn't know what was happening and the ED was happy to let it continue.

This is not a good place to be.

Re-engaging a disengaged board

Bringing a disengaged board back to the table takes a lot of small steps. Writing a monthly ED report, if you haven't already made it a habit, is a good place to start. *At least* you can bring them into the loop on what's happening.

The next task is to find small projects that give the board a win. Ask for help on something that is easily achievable.

Throwing this board into the deep end of the pool is a recipe for failure. But there are many ways they can help out and feel like they made a difference.

Can they make thank-you calls to donors *during the last ten minutes of the board meeting*? They can't get out of this! They are right there. But it will feel good. Here's another idea. Invite them to an event and "Stone Soup" it. Text, call, or email each board member and ask them to help out in some way. Can two serve wine? Can one bring a speaker system? Can the board president welcome people to the event? Can two board members volunteer to staff an information table?

Then, the day before the event, remind them what they volunteered to do.

You might get a couple cancellations. But, more often than not, they will come because they've made a *specific* commitment to help. This drives board attendance so much better than simply inviting the board to an event. Most of the time when you do that, a disengaged board will often skip. (Actually, this trick works well for any event where you want a critical mass of people to show up.)

Work hard on this kind of engagement a couple times and you'll start bringing a disengaged board back to the table.

You can also try inviting the board into your own brain, so to speak. You feel tension between competing goals. Like building reserves versus investing some of those dollars back in the program. Or serving a lot of people a little bit, or serving a small group really well. These are operational questions to a certain extent—you weigh questions like this every year on your own. But instead of doing that work in your own brain and coming to a conclusion, consider spelling it out for the board. Invite them into your brain. Because these are *meaty* topics that invite discussion about how the nonprofit should serve the public, and that can engage a board. The key is to find a range of possible outcomes you're comfortable with and then present those. You can facilitate a board discussion about them (or bring your board president in to facilitate the discussion) knowing that you are happy with any option. If the conversation becomes at all heated, you may be able to shut it down by thanking them for helping clarify your thinking about it and promising to report back.

Another good step to reengage a board is to try to arrange a half-day board retreat. Getting the board to plan, even if just for a few hours, should help reenergize them for the mission and the work. If you can afford a nonprofit facilitator, this is a great moment to bring them in.

Whatever comes of the retreat, do your best to help the board keep their commitments with the gentle nudges and helpful emails we've discussed.

Something to add is that this won't work with every board member. Some just might be truly checked out. In those situations, it should be obvious to the board president, but if it's not, I think it's appropriate to suggest that they get a message from the board president inviting them back. Something like: "We are starting some exciting new things and we've love to have your voice in the room! Would you still like to be on the board and help steer the ship?" This might bring them back but it might be a way to gently part.

That said, some boards might need to keep these folks "technically" on the board so they don't run afoul of their bylaws or shrink too much. If that's your situation, you'll want to act fast. Think of donors, community members, volunteers, strategic program partners, and more who might be interested in joining the board. See if you can get two to three to come on board at the same time. One may not fix your problem. But a small group, joining at the same time, can really energize a board. (For more on this, there's a whole chapter on board recruitment in *The Little Book of Boards*.)

Getting a micromanaging board to back off

It's easy for me to say, "A board should not run operations—that's your job." But if the board *expects* to sign off on a new brochure, if they *expect* to have input on hiring for junior positions, and if they *expect* to approve small operational changes, then what does it matter what I say? How do you get them to change so that they focus on the right things?

You can't just take something away (approving the brochure and other operational work) without having something meaningful for them to do. So that's the first step: ask a micromanaging board for help on something that is clearly in their realm.

For example:

"Our organization is at a real turning point, and I think we could all use more understanding of where we want to go. I'd like the board to consider launching a strategic planning process to help lay out a path for us over the next three years."

Or:

"I could really use some additional help on the fall fundraiser. I'm happy to do the grunt work, but I would love ideas and help setting the tone and direction, as well as getting people to attend."

You could also confide in the board president: "The board meetings are going really long. What would you think of working with the board to improve its committee structure so it can manage the workload a little better? I'm very happy to staff the committee meetings! This kind of a suggested change wouldn't be received as well if it came from me, but if you see merit there, I wonder if you could spearhead that."

So that's the first part. If you don't like the board micro-managing what is properly your responsibility, find somewhere else to point them. *Real* work. Work that a board *should* lead.

Then, once the board is engaged in that big project, that's the time to change how you present the operational work. In your ED report, for example, you might mention that the brochure will go to print the week after next and include an attachment of "the final version." It's not on the agenda, but at least they are seeing it in advance. So no one can say that you went rogue or took something from them that they felt like they should have input on.

Maybe no one will comment on the brochure! If so, you've set a new precedent. And if someone brings it up at the meeting, take notes and say you're happy to chat about it via phone or email the next day so you don't take time away from the busy agenda. Even in this situation, you may still end up engaging more than you would like with the one board member who really cares about this. But this is *so* much better than the alternative, where one passionate board member gets a discussion going, the entire board is pulled into it, sides get taken, and suddenly fifteen people are wordsmithing on the fly. If you can prevent that large-scale half-hour discussion from happening with the above steps, that's a big win for the entire board.

Then, next year, you could just send it to the one board member in advance, *or*—if things have gone well so far—just print it yourself. Ask for forgiveness, not permission.

Again, if you move to an "ask for forgiveness, not permission" model too fast, especially on topics where the board expects input, you can expect some pushback. So look for these opportunities to slowly move the board in such a way where they will pass off the responsibility more easily.

Know thyself (and know when to ask for help)

The key to making this work well, of course, is to effectively run the operations of the nonprofit! If the board isn't happy with some particular area of the nonprofit, they will want more information and oversight, regardless of whether it's "operations" or not.

The more trust you build up with the board, the more it's easy to say, "This was a one-off problem, I've addressed it, and it won't happen again." But if the brochure has glaring typos and pixelated photographs every year, then yeah—they're going to want to see it each time.

I said earlier that my directive to an Executive Director is to "know thyself" and it comes up again here. *Know* where you need help, even if it's related to operations, and ask for help in those areas. It's perfectly fine to ask a board member: "I'm a fast writer but I often skip important words. Would you be willing to look over my grant applications before they get sent out to catch typos?"

Or you might suggest to the board or the executive committee: "I'm not current on how to run a social media strategy. I'm going to use some of the professional development budget to enroll in a webinar about it. But in the meantime, can we form a small marketing committee to assist me in planning this for the year?"

This isn't weakness. It's not abdicating your job. It's being honest with the board (and yourself) about where you could use their help. The strategies above are for when you don't want a board butting in on areas where you think you have it well handled. But it's OK to lean on the board for the areas where you know you could use the support.

Supporting the board in their work

There are some core duties that fall to the board of a nonprofit. I cover them in the first chapter of *The Little Book of Boards* and earlier in this book I gave them each a bullet point when I described what an ED's job is. But I'm going to go through them here with a different lens. This time we'll talk about how you, the Executive Director, can best support your board in their work.

Boards ensure the nonprofit is following the mission.
    The board is accountable to the public (and specifically to the IRS in the United States) to make sure the organization is following its mission. It's important! Your role as the ED is to make sure you aren't bringing ideas or programs to them that are outside the mission. Don't go chasing money when it pulls you away from your mission.

    In addition, you may also see a business opportunity to expand, contract, or otherwise change the mission. In which case, that's a big process and it really should be board led, usually as part of a larger strategic planning or visioning process. But you could bring it to their attention during a retreat or through a relevant committee when appropriate.

Boards set policy.
    A board creates guidelines for how they want the nonprofit managed. This could mean cash-handling procedures, criteria for partnership, board policies about how they govern, sustainability policies, and more. Even an employee handbook, if it's been approved by the board, is a form of policy. The ED can help with research and first drafts when the board wants to

create new policies for something. If the finance committee is considering cash-handling rules, you can propose something—you, after all, will know best what is workable and what is not. For other policies, you might be the researcher who assembles two or three sample policies you find on the Internet and bring them to a committee for review.

Finally, the ED is likely the one to keep track of policies the board has adopted. Boards of small nonprofits often fall down on this part. They pass something, and then there's no centralized way to keep track of what they passed! The ED can keep a binder or a computer folder of all current policies or delegate the task to someone else on staff. Some nonprofits maintain a binder for each board member with bylaws, current policies, minutes of recent board meetings, and more. This is helpful (though a lot of work) and if it's more than you can manage, just store everything online in one central location like Google Drive or another online service. But the ED can definitely help keep these policies from falling through the cracks and saving everyone a lot of work. (It's dispiriting to everyone to spend a few meetings working on a new policy only to find out that you already had it on the books and everyone had just forgotten.)

It's worth noting that most boards do have a position to do this—the board secretary. But boards often don't think to empower that officer to do it. An ED can definitely work hand in hand with the board secretary or the chair of the governance committee to build the systems and then maintain them.

These documents should also go to new board members when they join!

Boards have oversight over finances.

A board should approve a budget and otherwise be informed about what's happening financially. Your best liaison here is the treasurer, or the entire finance committee if you have one. Regular reports should include at least two documents: a year-to-date profit and loss statement (either compared to the budget or compared to last year) and a balance sheet.

You can improve your reporting to the board in other ways as well. I'm a fan of a one-page dashboard that goes on top of the financial report. At the Grand we called it "ten important numbers." It was a sheet of key numbers next to the numbers we were comparing them to (an average, a budget, a goal, or whatever made the most sense for that indicator). Sometimes these numbers were financial and sometimes it was just a count, such as how many patrons came through the doors in the previous month. At City Club, the dashboard had six charts of information, such as number of current members. The charts fit on a single page and a board member could easily glance at them and get important information. These kinds of simple presentations are useful to a board member who doesn't feel confident understanding profit and loss reports or a balance sheet.

The other role when it comes to finances is that if the ED discovers a tight cash flow, they should keep the treasurer and finance committee informed. Sometimes I think about the treasurer as being the position to sound an alarm for the rest of the board if there's a financial issue. But it's even better to have the ED sound the alarm to the treasurer first.

Boards fundraise.

In theory, boards should be active in fundraising and often should be in the lead. But in my experience board members are usually wary of this. Many are scared of asking for money. Whenever I consult with a board that hasn't traditionally embraced fundraising, I usually advise getting specific in what the board members should commit to. For example, I might propose that everyone on the board gives a gift, everyone agrees to fill a table at an annual fundraiser (if they have one), and that everyone connects their friends and those in their circle to the nonprofit.

This is relatively light. But it's doable and meaningful. Everyone on a board should be able to do that.

Other board members might do more, such as serve on the committee to plan the fundraising event, and others may be tapped to call donors and thank them for their gift. Some might even ask for gifts themselves. But most should be able to commit to what's above.

Your role in supporting a board who is willing to participate in fundraising is to take care of the logistics. If there's a phon-a-thon, you should have the call sheets ready. If there's an event, you can get the catering bids and propose them to the committee. Use the board (or the committee) when you want a sounding board. Use them when many hands make light work (a board doing a phon-a-thon night can call many more numbers than a single person can). And use them for relationship building (the social network of a board is significantly larger than yours, just by virtue of their numbers). If you set the stage and make it as easy as possible for a board member to participate, you'll appreciate it.

Boards conduct long-range planning.

When a board and an ED have a high level of trust, they can really do great things. One of them is to sketch out a strategic plan. Where is the organization going? What is the community need? How is funding changing? How is technology changing? How can your organization skate to where the puck is going?

Some nonprofits use outside consultants for this, which is

definitely a good idea if you can afford it. But you don't always need to do that. If your nonprofit is embarking on this process without outside help, you might offer to write the first draft. After a board retreat or after a few meetings that discuss this, assemble the notes and put them together into something the board can review. After all, you will be the one to use it, so why not structure it in a way that's useful to you?

Aim for something short, just a few pages, that identifies the goal, why it's important, and how you think you'll get there. Things may change, but you'll do better if you plan for things instead of just react to things as they happen. And doing this as a group exercise will help make sure that you're canceling out each other's blind spots.

Your role is to be the "expert" in the room. You know the organization and you know the opportunities better than anyone. So you should most definitely be at the table and the board should turn to you often. But, in this case, you're also not the sole decider. Participate, give the information, and advocate for what you think. But it's not your way or the highway. It's the board's document, produced in collaboration with you.

Boards hire, fire, supervise, and evaluate the Executive Director.

Boards supervise and evaluate the ED—that's you! How best to assist them in that? (Besides doing a good job?) Well, that's the first thing you can do—you have to tell them about the job you're doing. Put it in writing. I said it earlier, but it bears repeating here: write a one to two page report every month about your work. If you don't tell them what you're doing, they'll make up an answer in their heads. Better to tell them!

There are other ways you can support this item.

Many EDs will ask for a performance review if the board isn't on top of it. It's not uncommon. In fact, most small nonprofits don't have a standardized way of doing performance reviews, so if you propose a way you'd like to be reviewed, you're likely to see it happen.

The other thing to point out here is that boards appreciate a lot of notice when you are ready to leave. I gave three months' notice when I left City Club of Tacoma and they still did not have an ED ready to go by the time I was gone. The process always seems to take longer than folks expect. So—if you can— that means giving more, maybe even up to six months or a year's notice. And yes, that's a lot of time! Some EDs give notice without knowing their next job. (In that way, giving a lot of notice helps the ED find their next job too. There's more about this in the appendix on letting go.)

Boards improve themselves.

I believe that boards should improve themselves over time.

One way I interpret this is that they should strategically recruit and gain stronger board members with more experience as the organization grows. You can support the board in this by identifying good candidates throughout the year and encouraging them to think about board service. Be clear that you are not in a position to install them on the board all by yourself. But if they are interested, offer to connect them to the board president or chair of the nominations committee. Think of good donors, community leaders, volunteers, and other folks who like the organization and who you already know you work well with. This will really help the board make sure they have new people on tap to fill vacancies. And there's another benefit to this, which is that as the board turns over, more and more board members will come in because they like and respect the work you are doing.

If the board governance committee or nominating

committee meets to discuss nominees, I would work to be in the room for that meeting as well. I urged you to be cautious in meddling in board business and that remains true. But if there is a candidate under consideration for the board who you have difficulty working with, I personally believe it is appropriate to share that. For example, "I respect the work that Alex does in the community tremendously, I really do. But I want to let you know that for some reason he and I have not had a good working relationship when our paths have crossed. I don't think it's anything about him—or me!—but our styles just haven't gelled very well in the past. I'm worried that it could cause some unnecessary internal strife."

You could also try to divert candidates like this to a committee if this first response doesn't sway the board. "Perhaps we could invite Alex to use his skills on the finance committee? If we get along well, then he could move to the board next year, but if it was clear we were butting heads, it might not be as much of an issue."

Most board members will appreciate knowing your feelings and will take it into account. Just know that some might indeed feel like you're meddling. I'll put it this way: if you are scrupulous about avoiding meddling in the board business, this is not a bad place to exert influence. No current board member should want to invite someone to join the board if they already have a difficult relationship with the ED. It's a recipe for a lot of fighting. But they won't know if you don't tell them. So pipe up here if needed.

"Improving itself" also means that boards should have opportunities for trainings, when appropriate. I've seen boards benefit from diversity training, public speaking training, fundraising coaching, retreat facilitation, "how to be a board member" training, and more. (I've led several of these trainings as well!)

It's a perk of being on a board—gaining new skills.

But sometimes it might feel weird to recommend to your boss(es) that they should get training. A good step is encouraging outside facilitation for your annual retreat. When the facilitator asks you and the executive committee what the board should work on, you can chime in with your experiences. That will help the facilitator better craft an agenda to move the board forward.

You can also alert the board to free resources when you find them. "Here's a free webinar about fundraising for anyone who is interested" is a nonthreatening way to approach it. And, if you are going to a conference or to a paid training, consider inviting board members to attend with you. "I'm going to the all-day Philanthropy Summit next month and registration closes next week. If any board member would care to attend, let me know and we can plan our day together!"

Committee chairs are also good conduits. Send a fundraising training to the development committee chair and you can bet it will go to the full committee or board.

Help the board use its muscles (so they don't atrophy)

There's an old saying that character is revealed in great moments, but it is made in small ones. Think about your board in a similar way. Many board procedures feel like "extra work." Or they don't seem efficient. But they are practice for bigger moments. They build relationships of trust and they build routines. When there's a crisis—or an opportunity!—the board will be better prepared to handle it.

An executive committee that meets quarterly will be better prepared to meet at the drop of a hat and actually do the important work than an executive committee that has never met before. And on and on. These things take practice.

Your job as an ED is to do your best to keep the train on the tracks. Use gentle nudges and make it as easy as possible for the board to do their work. It will go a long way.

"Whoever shows up with the agenda wins"

When I became senior patrol leader in Boy Scouts, I had to run my first meeting. I was probably in late middle school, maybe early high school, and the meeting would have both adults and scouts. I'd never led a meeting before and my dad gave me an important piece of advice: "Whoever shows up with the agenda wins." I've found that it is still true to this day. (Yes, "wins" is a really interesting word if you think about it. If you don't want to see the world in that competitive light, I get it. But my dad was right. There's opportunity there, if you want to reach for it.)

Showing up with an agenda—even if it clearly says DRAFT at the top—means the meeting will almost certainly unfold along the lines of your agenda. Blank pages can be daunting and people appreciate having some structure. Sure, the agenda might change a bit here and there based on what other people want to talk about, but mostly, it's a good way to focus a group on what you'd like them to address.

It's a thumb on the scale that you, the ED, can choose to use.

I've used it when I've asked the executive committee to meet: "Here are some things we need to get through today. Am I missing anything?"

I've used it with the board president: "I've talked to the committee chairs, and here's what I expect we need to get through at the board meeting next week. Do you have additions or changes?"

Instead of merely hoping that the board deals with a particular topic, this is a really useful way to make sure it gets handled.

Now, if you abuse this power, you'll get called out on it. But if you use it to help the board keep the promises that they've made to themselves already, you shouldn't get any pushback.

Use the executive committee

My other secret weapon for getting the most from the board is to activate the executive committee. This committee is usually made up of the board officers—the president, vice president, secretary, and treasurer for example. Sometimes the past president may serve on the committee as well. In other words, it's a committee of the board's elected leadership.

Asking for a meeting every other month, or quarterly, is a good way to get a key group of board members together regularly. A quarterly executive committee meeting can help plan the next three months of agendas. They can sketch out a rough draft of what needs to be covered and then you and the board president can hone each month's specific agenda based on how the work has actually gone.

This is also a good group to bring up what you'd like to see happen, such as getting a board retreat on the calendar, or asking for a performance review.

Boards who don't have a cultural expectation of having an executive committee might need a gentle nudge. Maybe invite them together for a one-off meeting that has a specific focus, and when they are there you can also suggest they talk about the next few months of agendas. "It won't take long, but the planning will help" sort of thing. Either at that meeting or in a few months, propose getting together again and suggest it could become a regular meeting.

It works!

Things to watch for

I'd like to finish this section on getting the most out of your board by identifying some things to watch for—both within yourself and the board. As I keep saying, the relationship between the board and the ED can be a strange one. Here are some things I've observed in my time:

What should rise to the level of board attention?

There's a sweet spot for an ED where you manage the operations, keep the board informed of the important decisions and information, while also *not* bringing every little detail or issue to their attention. It's a tricky balance, and you are liable to get some of it wrong here and there. Or, perhaps, not *wrong* per se, but your view of that balancing act will differ from a board member's view.

Let's look at a quick series of problems:

1. *Does the board need to know that there was a billing error with your mailing list software that caused you to have to delay the monthly newsletter a week?* No, definitely not. This is entirely an operations issue.
2. *Does the board need to know that the error caused your account to close for a few weeks, and you had to reestablish your list from old data, meaning you had lost the names and email addresses of the last one hundred newsletter subscribers?* No, probably not. Unless you are looking for some things to pad out your report, this is entirely an operations issue, and not even a very serious one.
3. *Does the board need to know that this billing error was a result of the account being flagged for sending*

spam and that to address the issue will cost $500?
Yes, probably the board does need to know this. But
depending on your budget size, it might be a
paragraph in your ED report (if $500 is a lot for
you) or it might be simply a single-sentence bullet
toward the end of your report (if that's a small part
of your tech budget). Depending on the speed that
you can address it, you might be able to present this
as something that's already been fixed—which is
usually the best way to present any "negative" news
like this—or something that will be fixed soon,
which is also fine.

4. *Does the board need to know that the error resulted
in revealing credit card information for your
members—even if there's no evidence that anyone
took it or stole that data?* OMG YES, the board
needs to know it. This has the potential for a large
financial implication to the organization, there are
reputational issues, donor relationship issues, and
maybe even state laws. This is a big deal.

When I lay it out like this, it's easy to see the progression.
But it may not feel like it when you are the ED. Emotionally, it's
going to be tempting to treat the worst item like the easiest item
and *not* bring it to the board's attention.

I know, because I've done it. And it absolutely blew up in
my face.

Here's what happened: At City Club, I received a notice
that—before my time as ED—the nonprofit had incorrectly paid
payroll taxes. To make the account right, the IRS had sent a
large bill, something like $5,000 if I remember correctly. At the
time, funds were low, the board was wrangling over something
or other, and I felt like things were hard enough on them at that

moment. I thought: *I can deal with this. They don't need to be bothered.* I thought I knew a few ways to deal with it. I tried those ideas for a few months, they didn't work, and so I took the issue to the board.

That's when it blew up.

Can you spot the problem? The initial error wasn't mine—it predated my time as ED. And I brought it to the board of my own volition. So those weren't the sticking points. It was this bit: "I tried those ideas for a few months." In other words, I didn't tell the board about a major and unexpected bill. For months.

Even if I thought I could handle it on my own, I absolutely should have included it in my ED report or in a conversation with the board president or executive committee. The omission was the problem, not the bill itself.

This was an error in *judgment*. And if an ED is hired to make decisions, as I say in the early chapters, then errors in judgment about large numbers are very concerning to a board.

If you're staring at something that might be a big problem and trying to decide if or when to bring it to the board, here are the three questions you should ask yourself:

How confident are you that you can solve it within a couple weeks?

If you can solve it within a couple weeks, then you can bring a problem to the board that you've also fixed, which is nice. But if it's big enough that you can't solve it before the next board meeting, that's a good sign that you need to inform them of it.

What are the worst possible downsides?

If the problem has a high financial cost or a high reputational cost, that's a good sign you should inform the board.

How well do you know how to fix the problem on your own?

To use the example above, if I ran a nonprofit that had a possible leak of credit card data, I would need a lot of outside help on how to appropriately handle that situation. I wouldn't know the legal responsibilities of a nonprofit in that situation and I would want outside communications expertise on how to manage any fallout from donors.

Similarly, I didn't know how to solve the tax bill problem at City Club. I was hoping some ideas would work, but I didn't really know. And by trying to "go it alone" I compounded my error by not getting help from people who actually knew how to handle it. Once the board was able to process their surprise and disappointment with how I'd handled it, it turned out that they knew much better than I did how to deal with it. I should have started there.

Again, sometimes you're going to make mistakes in the balance between managing operations and informing the board. But hopefully you can learn from my experience and only make this mistake on smaller things.

Boards are usually reluctant to fire their EDs

Even in the case of big mistakes like mine, here's some good news. In general, boards don't like to fire their Executive Directors. For one, it causes a huge amount of work for them, and they will usually be reluctant to take this step unless they feel like they absolutely have to. They might worry about how something like this will look or its effect on the staff. In addition, if anyone on the board participated in hiring the ED, they might feel that firing the ED represents a failure on their part.

But the real reason boards are often reluctant to do this is that everyone on the board has a different experience with the concept of what it means to fire someone. Some may have been fired and can't imagine putting someone else through it. Some may have a relationship with the ED and would never fire their friend. Some may expect a laborious process before termination. So it's hard to get a group of people to agree when they all come from different backgrounds.

That doesn't mean it can't happen, of course. Plenty of EDs *are* fired. I've talked about examples in this book even. But I flag it here because I want to urge you: Don't be too worried about honest mistakes, especially if you work to avoid making the same mistake over and over. And don't be afraid of standing up for yourself and what you believe either. If you are doing your job to the best of your abilities, if you are clear with yourself and the board about where you need help, then having a little backbone is not going to be the end of the world.

It's another reason why I advocate asking for forgiveness instead of asking for permission. Do the job and own up to mistakes when they happen. Assume leadership, and you will likely get it.

Board bullies

Unfortunately, sometimes being the loudest person in the room works. If a board member is displaying toxic behavior, it can cause real issues at the organization in terms of board morale and even operations (as the board might cave on something they shouldn't just to pacify the bullying board member).

It is incredibly difficult to handle a toxic board member because (often) no one really wants to put up a fight. In those cases, they'd rather try to find compromises or just give in to the bully. I've even seen attempts by boards to put this person in a leadership position, hoping that will soften the bully (it hasn't worked so far as I can see).

No one has to be there

One of the reasons bullies are a problem at small nonprofits is because of this core truth: no one has to be there. Even for the most committed and dedicated board member, it's still not their actual job. If the experience of being on the board is toxic, painful, or the worst of all chores, then they are going to look for an exit ramp.

I saw a board with a toxic board member on it. The board meetings were tense and no one wanted to speak up. Over the course of two or three years, not a single person renewed their board term, and many left early, citing family, work, and other reasons. All of the reasons were technically valid and I've seen board members step down for those reasons in other contexts and didn't think anything of it. But add them all up and it was clear that the board members just didn't want to put up with the toxic board member anymore.

This is a dangerous place to be for a nonprofit and it's a big challenge for the board to address. But it's not just a challenge to them, it can be a problem for you too.

What happens when you are the target of the bully?

As usual, I think it's worth talking to your board president first. You've probably commiserated about this board member already. But if you feel it has crossed a line beyond just dealing with a difficult personality, then the correct workplace procedure is to talk about it with your supervisor. Use the word *bullying*. Document and describe the behavior.

If the board president is the problem, or part of the problem, the vice president or another officer might be a good place to start instead.

Unfortunately, though, describing bullying rarely captures the sensation of actually being bullied. It's not uncommon for a description of bullying to sound tame to someone who doesn't "get it." So send links to online resources about workplace bullying if the board president or executive committee don't have experience in this area. Whether or not any action is taken, you have given notice that the board member has become a problem for you in your workplace.

You can also work to limit your contact with the bully. For example, if you find yourself getting called into long, toxic phone calls with this board member, let me be the first to tell you: you don't have to pick up. You don't work for the bully, you work for the board and the committees you "staff." There's nothing in your job description that says you have to take ninety-minute phone calls and miss dinner with your family. You could reply via email the next day with something like: "I'm very happy to respond to your emails and work with you on committees and on the board, but I don't have the time available for long phone conversations right now. Thanks for your understanding. What's up?"

This might get a bully angry and kick off a confrontation. But if I've learned anything about bullies on the board it's that these scenes are inevitable. Stand your ground and try not to lose your cool.

At some point, someone has to confront the situation with a bully. You never know what will spark it—perhaps it's your email, perhaps it's someone else on the board.

Pay attention to culture

With that in mind, I think it's important that the ED pay attention to the board culture. Is there camaraderie on the board? Are there lots of hugs and smiles?

Or, on the other hand, are there meetings in the parking lot afterward where the "real meeting" takes place? Is there constant backbiting?

As the ED, you are a witness to the culture and you can have some influence on it. But you are also a step removed from it. You can use that to hold up a mirror for the board. At an executive committee meeting, you can share your observations. This is like calling out the elephant in the room: "I'm seeing a lot of anger over the budget process that feels like it's really anger about other issues and they are just playing themselves out here. There seem to be factions and cliques and side conversations that I don't always understand. I don't know the answer, but I wanted to share what I'm seeing." It might start the committee on a path toward addressing it.

The answer to bad board culture is often *sunlight* or *time*.

A skilled facilitator at a retreat can tease these issues out and deal with them in the open. Sunlight is a great cure for a lot of these issues and open conversations about them—often with good facilitation—can leave everyone feeling a lot better.

The other solution is time. "Time heals all wounds," as they say. But there's another way that time can help a board culture —time simply spent together as a full board. Boards benefit from time together, especially some time outside of meetings. On one board I've served, we've made (and then eaten) meals together. What a joy to work together in that way.

One tradition I recommend is that a board have a social meeting or activity at least once a year. Here's something I've done several times—hold an annual orientation for new board members. These usually run ninety minutes at most. Cover the key information a new board member will want to know. Then, immediately after, transition to a happy hour or social with the rest of the board. It's a "Welcome to the Board" party! It's an inviting welcome to the new board members, and it's a chance for the current board to see each other when they aren't just across the boardroom table.

You can also help build board culture by engaging them as a group (or as several small groups) with the mission. What if the board took a shift as volunteers together a couple times a year? Or invite them to the cast party after the play. Cook a meal together after a meeting! These touches outside of board meetings are vitally important. You can help facilitate them or recommend them to the executive committee.

It's not necessarily on you

Once, as an ED, I was struggling with the board dynamic I saw at meetings. It felt tense and I worked hard to manage the nonprofit as well as I possibly could, hoping that it would relieve the tension. I told myself that I could fix things. I thought it would be better "if I can just get more money in the bank..." or "if I can improve my membership numbers..."

What I especially remember about this was that one month I had an absolutely amazing report in every single way. Everything was going great. We had big new sponsors, lots of money in the bank, and new exciting stuff. I felt good going into that board meeting. And I expected to see a lighter mood as a result.

I was wrong. The same tension persisted.

I couldn't fix the problem that way, because I'd misread it. It was never about the numbers or my performance. Sometimes the issues aren't about the specifics of the nonprofit, even though it can feel like it. Sometimes it's the relationships and the emotions. I've seen successful nonprofits with board infighting, and I've seen struggling nonprofits with real board unity. Don't put a dysfunctional board dynamic on your shoulders—there are ways you can help, as I've talked about. But it's not something that you can always manage from your position.

Don't be a sore loser

The Executive Director is the expert in the nonprofit and how it functions. But on some issues, the ED isn't the decision-maker. That means that sometimes the ED will lose. Sometimes you'll have a great new idea and work hard to make it happen, only to find it's a non-starter with the board.

I've been there. It sucks, I'll be perfectly honest.

The best thing to do is to chalk it up as a loss and move on.

Change is measured in years at a nonprofit. You might come to appreciate the board's position. Or you might find a better opportunity to present your idea later when the board makeup has changed.

There's no truly "done" when it comes to nonprofit work. (It's actually one of the hardest things about the job, to be honest.) But there is a "done for now." Put a pin in it, give it some time, and if you still care about your idea, you will find a way to bring it back later.

Tug-of-war

As a final thought for this chapter, there's an old piece of advice that I find to be true in a variety of situations: If you want someone to change how they treat you, change how you treat them. Want someone to be kinder to you? Be kind to them. Want someone to treat you more professionally? Treat them more professionally first. And so on.

I'll be the first to say that this can take a while! But it's a useful lens for thinking about your relationship with the board as a whole. If you want the board to change and grow, you will have to change and grow too.

Here's another way to envision it.

Let's imagine you and the board are engaged in a tug-of-war: you on one side, and the board on the other. It's not that there's an adversarial relationship, but there's a little tension. The rope is always taut.

What are your options if you want to change what's happening on the board's side?

Well, you can't *push* the board to do anything for the simple reason that you can't push a rope. So where does that leave you?

You could pull harder, but it's you against several more people. You're going to lose eventually (and burn yourself out in the process).

You could let go. Which changes the board, certainly! By making them stumble and go into disarray. This is what happens when an Executive Director gives up on the board, or —after months or years of frustration—dumps a problem in the board's lap that they aren't prepared for.

Or you can play the game of tug-of-war, without playing to *win*. You keep the rope taut but take small steps forward or backward depending on which way the board needs to go. They will move with you because the rope is taut. Small steps, small changes.

If you want your board to do more work (strategic planning, fundraising, financial oversight, etc.) then slowly step closer to them, give them a little rope, and let them take up the slack. It means not trying to control how they do it, because that is something they are going to take care of on their side of the rope. But you can give them space to work and gentle nudges to keep them on track.

If you want your board to be willing to give you more work (daily operations, marketing, etc.) then slowly step back with gentle pressure. Take on a little more responsibility here and there. When the board wants something done, volunteer to write the first draft and implementation plan. Slowly but surely, you'll get the responsibility you need to run the organization.

SEVEN

ASKING YOUR BOARD FOR A RAISE

LET'S fast-forward on Linda's story by a couple years.

After three years on the job, and after her hard work to increase the budget of the Historical Society by more than forty percent, Linda started to realize that she wanted to make more too. She wanted to buy a new home. She wanted to afford a long vacation somewhere hot and relaxing. She wanted some nicer things around the house.

And she realized that, in some subtle way, she wasn't feeling valued by her board anymore. A few weeks before, a job at the state historical society opened up that Linda was easily qualified for. The pay was $20,000 more a year than Linda made now! Sure, some of that was because it was in the big city where salaries were always higher than in Smallville. But the nonprofit wasn't substantially bigger than the Smallville Historical Society and if Linda were willing to commute forty minutes each way, it would be a huge financial win for her.

Except she *didn't* want to commute, that's why she took the job at the Smallville Historical Society in the first place. She wanted to stay in her community. She just wanted to earn more money. It didn't have to be $20,000 more (it almost certainly wouldn't be) but earning something closer to that would be meaningful.

So how to go about asking? Would the board be angry that she asked? Could the Smallville Historical Society even afford a raise? Linda wasn't sure where to start. Before working in nonprofits, she had worked at an insurance company. While there, she'd asked for (and gotten) two raises. But that felt different than this problem. It had been hard enough to get just one boss to approve a raise, but now she had eleven people who would have to agree. It seemed too daunting.

After thinking about it for a while, she realized there was even a *downside* to getting a raise. It was weird to think that there was a downside to making more money, but it was true: the board had hired Linda to manage the budget. If they gave her a raise it was just going to add to the expense line of the nonprofit. Her job would become slightly more difficult!

There was another part of it that was hard to think about. When she sat down with major donors and asked for $5,000 or $10,000, she could tell them exactly how their gift would help fund the Historical Society's youth education programs. And it would! She knew how she could put that money into a program budget so that kids and the mission would benefit. Asking the board for that $5,000 or $10,000 to go to her personally instead of the nonprofit's programs felt almost...selfish?

And yet, when she was being honest with herself, she knew she wanted it. And she felt like she probably deserved it too.

Linda is not alone in her anxiety around compensation. *Many* leaders at small nonprofits wrestle with these issues around their own compensation. Let's break it down. Here's the Five Ws (the Who, What, Where, When, Why, and How?) of asking for a raise—though I'm going to tackle it in an order that makes more sense.

Why should you ask for a raise?

Besides the fact that you just want more money, I mean. Let's dive in.

First, you deserve to be paid what you are worth.

Unapologetically. That should be your mental starting point. Sometimes there's a temptation to hem and haw about this and say, "But I love the mission! I don't want to take away from it. I'll just make less."

In some ways, though, that feeling is already priced into a nonprofit ED's salary. Having a job with a cause or a mission you are passionate about is worth something. A nonprofit Executive Director's salary (especially at a small nonprofit) usually pays less than similar positions at for-profit businesses. This is part of the reason why.

In fact, there are other intangibles associated with working at a nonprofit, especially in the position of Executive Director:

- Often there's greater flexibility than at a for-profit business.
- You can build your skills or personal network in a way that will reward you at a future job.
- The work environment or work/life balance can be better at a nonprofit.

But after taking all those factors into account, you should *still* get paid what you're worth. If you could make $90,000 at a for-profit, but are making $70,000 at a nonprofit, the trade-off for significantly better quality of life might be worth it. But if you could make $90,000 at a for-profit and are only making

$45,000 at a nonprofit, that's not a great trade-off, no matter the intangible benefits.

You deserve to make what you're worth.

Second, the role of Executive Director is key to implementing the mission.

Linda felt like she had to make a choice between asking the board for a raise and using those funds for the program. But usually, that's a false choice at a small nonprofit. If you are the ED at a small nonprofit, you are a key part of the program. You can't separate them at this small of a scale. If you are writing grants, asking donors for money, or directly supervising the staff member or volunteers who are leading the program, the ED is not separate from the work of the nonprofit! This role is very much a part of it.

To better illustrate what I mean, imagine what the nonprofit would do if you left suddenly and the organization had to go four or six months before hiring your replacement. Relationships with donors and partners would weaken. Grants might not get written. Staff might lose focus. The overall mission and financial health of the organization would suffer.

In other words: if you are underpaid and starting to think of greener pastures, paying you a higher salary is in the best interest of the nonprofit and in the best interest of the mission.

Third, the job of ED is different than a lower-level job at the same nonprofit.

If your marketing coordinator quits, you can find another marketing coordinator for roughly the same pay who will do roughly the same work. (I chose that title because I was once a marketing coordinator and I didn't want to talk badly about someone else's job. Sorry, fellow marketing coordinators.)

For the Executive Director, though, it's much different. Change the leader and the ramifications will be felt from the top of the organization to the bottom. As a board member, I've hired an Executive Director. And the job qualifications are just the first level of assessing a candidate for the position. After that, the board looks for a match to the vision, strategic direction, prior relationships, and much more. Executive Directors are not interchangeable cogs. That means that if you leave your job, by default, the organization will look different under a new leader. If there is a vision for the organization that you and the board agree on, and things are working well in pursuit of that vision, then (again) it's in the nonprofit's best interest to pay you what you're worth.

I'll repeat it. *You deserve to make what you're worth.* It's good for you, and it's good for the organization.

Who should you ask?

Normally, I'm the guy who wants you to run everything by your board president first. Ninety-nine percent of the time, that's the right move. But I think that's a mistake here. Why? Because it puts a lot of power into one person's hands. Salary and compensation are the *full* board's responsibility. That means if the board president has any hang-ups about your raise, he or she can effectively kill it on the spot, without any consultation with the rest of the board.

"Hang-ups?" I hear you ask. Sure. Board presidents are people too, and the same hang-ups we all have about money in our personal life can come to the table during these discussions.

The board president might not understand the budget very well, and any increase in expenses sounds scary. The board president might work at an institution like a hospital or university where the pay scale is highly regimented and is based on years of work and educational degrees. That kind of grid rarely works in a small nonprofit, but it can color a board member's thinking around your salary and request for a raise.

Another thing that can happen is this: the board president might make *less* than the Executive Director. Think about that for a second. At a nonprofit, an employee can make more than one of her supervisors. It's something that almost *never* happens in the for-profit world, but it is not uncommon in the nonprofit world with the ED/board relationship. As a board member, I have made less in my regular job than the ED I supervised and as an ED, I've made more than some board members.

All of these hang-ups can be addressed in a group setting where (ideally) the wisdom of crowds will prevail and they can get past any one individual board member's hang-ups.

Do you see the rub here? If the board president has any of these hang-ups, there's no other board member to talk her down from the ledge in a one-on-one meeting. It's just you and the board president.

So, if you bring your request to the board president first, and you get shot down, you've got two options in front of you—both poor. You can go around the board president and ask the full board for a raise (which could damage your relationship with the board president). Or you can just accept that you're not getting a raise. Neither will feel good.

So, again, who should you ask?

In my opinion, you should ask the executive committee.

Here's my argument:

You work for the board as a whole, not any one member, including the board president. But asking the entire board without any preamble might be...daunting. Boards don't like to be surprised, which is why we usually run things by the board president first. Plus, it's hard enough asking one person for a raise, but try asking fifteen of them!

But the executive committee (your board president, treasurer, VP, and secretary) is a likely first stop to hear about anything related to "personnel," which includes this. Even if your bylaws don't specifically call this "personnel" role out, that's fine. Taking this request to the executive committee will at least give you a good read on how the full board will react to the idea.

There's another benefit to taking it to the executive committee first: the treasurer is on the committee, which means that she can talk about finances if the question arises about "what the nonprofit can afford." If you've done a good job managing finances and working with the treasurer, this person should be a good advocate for you—or, *at least*, make it clear that the money is there.

Finally, the last benefit of taking this to the executive committee is that if you succeed in convincing them to recommend this to the full board, now you have four advocates on your side, and not just the one advocate you would have had if you'd asked only your board president.

For all these reasons, I believe the executive committee is the place to start.

When should you ask for a raise?

My vote: the middle of the fiscal year. If your budget runs January to December, ask in June. If your budget runs July to June, ask in January. Asking mid-fiscal year gives you a couple of advantages.

The first is that if you are having a great year so far, that's already clear and it's way easier for the board to approve the raise. To boards, a budget can often feel uncertain, especially if it projects increased revenues. If you ask for a raise during the budgeting process, you will probably get something like, "Let's see how the first few months go." By midyear, you and the board know how things are going.

The other reason is that asking midyear gives you the option to ask for a raise that will be effective at the start of the next fiscal year. Now, in an ideal world, your nonprofit would be doing so well financially they would just pay you more when you ask for it. But when it's not an ideal world—which is most of the time—this delay can help. If things at the nonprofit are good, but not great, having the board approve a raise a few months in advance will be easier for them to handle. Asking midyear also means you are almost certainly asking before you are crafting the next year's budget. That gives you and the board time to plan for this increase.

There's another subset of the "when" question. When should you ask for a raise *in relation to the health of the organization?*

If you are constantly unsure how you are going to make payroll, then it's a bad time to ask for a raise. Fix that first. Whatever the size of your budget, get a month or two of reserves in the bank. *Then* ask for a raise. Don't ask for a raise the nonprofit can't afford. You know the budget. You know what can be managed.

Where should you ask for a raise?

This isn't a real question anyone actually asks, but since I set this up as a "Who, What, Where, When, Why, How" of raises, I feel that I must include it.

So, where should you ask for a raise? You should ask in person. (I guess that's sort of "where," right?) Don't email the executive committee in advance with your request either. Get them in a room together and ask them there. This will give you the best opportunity to advocate on your behalf and answer objections.

What should you ask for?

This is the big question, right? Where the money really hits the road (or something like that). *How much of a raise should you ask for?*

There are a variety of factors that come into play here. And you're going to need to do some figuring on your end to justify what you want to the board. But I'm just going to make this easy on you and say you should ask for a ten percent raise.

Boom. Done. Next question.

Oh, you want more information than that?

Ok. Here's my argument:

First, if you ask for more than ten percent you need to have a really, really good reason why.

If you're making $50,000 a year, and you ask for a raise to $70,000, that's a forty percent raise. You will need a ton of supporting information for why this is a good idea, and your nonprofit will need to be really killing it in order to justify that added expense. It's certainly possible that a nonprofit that is going through a period of tremendous growth could make a leap like this. But for others with more stable revenues, without some larger rationale, I don't see a board going for it.

Now, if you still want to get from $50,000 to $70,000 you could present a compensation plan that lays out certain bench-marks (like money in the bank or other tangible and measurable goals) that will bump you up to $70,000 in the span of three or four years. But let's stick to just a single raise for now.

Usually, asking for a huge increase won't get you where you want. If you really think you deserve a forty percent pay increase immediately, you should probably just look for a new job rather than ask for the raise.

Second, if you ask for less than ten percent...you just might get it!

Asking for $52,000 when you make $50,000 is a four percent raise. And it's just not that much of a difference. When you divide a pay increase like that by twenty-four or twenty-six pay periods in a year, you may not even feel it.

Getting a bump of one, two, or three percent per year should be standard. It's called a COLA (short for Cost of Living Adjustment). Maybe your small nonprofit doesn't use COLAs. You should, but it's not uncommon for a small nonprofit to be so hand-to-mouth that even this is a hard thing to budget for. But even if you don't have a COLA, this should give you good context. Getting an additional two percent is not a raise, it's a COLA. If you treat it like a raise, you are wasting a lot of effort for very little money.

Third, you need to leave room for your board to negotiate.

In the same vein as above, you want a raise that is meaningful to you, even if the board won't agree to the full amount you ask for. If you ask for five percent and get three percent, that's not a raise you're going to actually feel. But if you ask for a ten percent raise and the board puts together a counteroffer for a six percent raise, that's not a terrible result. If you're going to go through the trouble of asking for a raise, ask for enough to make it worthwhile.

Ten percent is a good place to start.

A caveat

There's one caveat to the above advice. The smaller the salary, the more you should consider asking for a raise to the next round number, rather than ten percent.

Here's an example. If you're making $30,000, a bump to $33,000 isn't that much, even if it's ten percent. But asking to get up to $35,000 or $40,000 is a real increase. If you have the funds to manage a $5,000 or $10,000, then it's worth asking to be bumped up to the next plateau.

Watch out for compensation switches

It's important that you understand your full compensation package. Does your nonprofit pay your health care? Do they have a good vacation or sick leave policy? Do they chip into a retirement account on your behalf? Is there an automatic COLA?

You can certainly ask for these things along with a raise. But be warned that nonprofits love to give more vacation days because it's "free" for them. In my first job out of college, I had just finished a major initiative as marketing coordinator. I asked for a fifty-cent-per-hour raise (an incredibly small amount of money—my admonishment to ask for ten percent comes from my lived experience) and a title change. You can guess which one I got. I walked out of my boss's office a marketing manager, with no additional money in my pocket to show for it.

As a nonprofit grows and stabilizes, adding retirement matching, generous vacation, or automatic COLAs might be in your future. But I would get your salary up to something close to your understanding of "market level" before you start asking for these other benefits.

How should you ask for a raise?

First, do your research! What do other Executive Directors of nonprofits like yours make? You can find this out in a few ways.

The easiest is just looking it up on Guidestar.org. On Guidestar, search for local nonprofits of a similar size to yours and look for their most recent 990 form. It may be a year or two out of date, but you'll get a good sense of what similar organizations are paying.

You can also buy a "compensation report" from Guidestar, which is pulled from all the 990 forms they collect. A recent report was almost four hundred dollars, so it's not cheap. (But if it helps you get another $5,000 a year it may also be money well-spent!)

Some states also assemble this data based on job titles and you can find compensation reports there (though keep in mind the title Executive Director can be held by people who run credit unions, nursing homes, and other organizations that might be significantly different than yours).

External research completed, you should have a good idea of what "market rate" is. You'll want this data either for your own confidence or for presenting it to the board. But there's another kind of research you will want to do as well: research into the health of your own organization. If you want to earn another ten percent, can you afford it?

You can do this on your own, but you can even (slyly) bring your treasurer into the conversation. Let's say you wanted a $5,000/year raise. At a finance committee meeting, you might ask, "Thinking ahead, I know that we have three months' reserves. But how would we be looking if one of our expenses went up? Like if our rent or our insurance increased by $500/month? Could we still get by?" That discussion might shed some light on the topic for you.

Research in hand, you now can turn to the messaging. What do you tell the board? What's the argument? Well, your goal is to emphasize how this pay increase will help the nonprofit. Paying you more helps the nonprofit. *That's* the sell.

(This is where the advice that applies to asking for a raise at a for-profit *does* overlap with the advice for a nonprofit. You need to put forward a case for a raise that is more than just about putting money in your own pocket.)

I've mentioned two arguments already, but I'll repeat them here for clarity:

1. The current organization is a reflection of your skill as a manager and leader.

Assuming that the organization is healthy, it is in the nonprofit's best interest to pay you commensurate with your skills so that you can continue to lead the organization.

2. As the keeper and implementer of the vision of the nonprofit, investing in you ensures the progress you've made on your mission "sticks."

We've all seen nonprofits that change EDs every two or three years and every time there's a change the organization goes through a certain whiplash. Keeping a leader around longer prevents this.

There are other arguments you can make as well.

3. Relationships with donors take time to form, which means that keeping you as the ED will keep your relationships with donors strong.

This is a close argument to number two, but it's worth

teasing out separately. Individual giving and major giving takes highly relational work. If you were successful in asking for and receiving $1,000 from a major donor three years ago, $2,500 two years ago, and $5,000 last year, *only you* are going to be able to ask that donor for $10,000 this year. A new Executive Director, without the prior relationship, would be lucky just to keep that donor at $5,000. And even then...what if they don't connect? What if the rapport you have with that donor isn't there with the new ED? These kinds of things happen. Part of your value comes in the relationships that you have formed with donors. No matter how good you are at keeping your database up-to-date (and you should be!) a new ED can't replicate your solid relationships immediately. That is part of your value to the organization. If your organization can't keep an ED longer than three years, the relationships cultivated with your largest donors will never pay off.

4. Paying you more helps keep the entire staff at market rate.

The pay scale starts at the top. If you're making $50,000, you are going to have to find a program administrator who will earn less pay than you do. But if the market for someone with that title is higher, you're going to have a hard time finding a quality candidate to take that job. You might find someone young who you are taking a chance on (to be fair, that's how I got into nonprofit work!) but it's still a chance. If they don't perform, that's obviously not good. And if they *do* perform, they'll take their skills elsewhere fairly quickly.

If you want to pay your staff appropriately, your own salary needs to be set high enough to make room for them. In other words: your own salary is linked to the health of the organization!

. . .

5. The next ED will expect to make more.

This might surprise you so here's the argument spelled out as you might present it: "I want to be here for a long time, so don't get scared," you might say with a smile. "But to be frank, if I got hit by a bus tomorrow, you would have a hard time finding a high-quality candidate to accept the job for the current pay. If we increase my pay by ten percent now to get it closer to market rate, and then plan for smaller annual adjustments after that, it will mean that if I ever do get hit by that proverbial bus and you have to hire a new Executive Director, you won't have sticker shock all at once." Nonprofit boards shouldn't take their leaders for granted. And yet they often do, by paying the Executive Director poorly, and only belatedly realize they need to increase the pay when it's time to hire the new ED.

6. Funders expect it.

Well, to be clear they don't expect you to get a raise. (How nice would that be?!) But they do know what a healthy nonprofit should look like. Sustainable wages are as much a part of that measure as the amount of reserves you have in the bank. If you are reliant on foundation grants, they're not looking for a nonprofit that has slashed expenses to the bone. They're looking for a program that can be replicated from one year to another. And if the nonprofit is paying wages significantly below similar nonprofits, that's not a sustainable model for the people who serve. Funders know that.

Not every argument above will appeal to you or to your board. You'll know best which of them will fit your nonprofit's specific context. And there might be more arguments that apply to you than what I've covered! The most important thing is to frame your pay increase as something that will help the organization move forward. It's good for you *and* it's good for them. Show them that.

Back to Linda's raise

The executive committee of the Smallville Historical Society had fallen out of the practice of their quarterly meetings. So, Linda suggested to the board president that they get a meeting on the calendar to do some planning for the upcoming board retreat. She typed up an agenda and added an item at the end labeled "personnel" before sending it out. When the committee met and got to that final item on the agenda, all eyes turned to her.

"I added this agenda item because I wanted to bring up an important question that I felt I should discuss with the executive committee first. Over the past three years, the Historical Society has made some real gains. Our budget is up seventy percent since I started. We went from an ED and two part-time staff members to three full-time employees and one part-time. And on top of that, we have three months of reserves in the bank. I've been very proud to lead the organization." Linda took a breath and then repeated her memorized opener. "Given all that, I'd like to ask the board to consider an increase in compensation for my position. I've put together a proposal for your review." (At this point, Linda distributed a packet.) "As you can see, I'm looking for a ten percent increase in pay, from $65,000 to $71,500. I'd also like us to budget for an automatic two percent cost-of-living adjustment for myself and all staff members at the end of each fiscal year. In fact, the staff is one of the reasons I'm requesting this. Organization-wide, we need to be ready to pay higher wages to keep the team that I've assembled. We haven't increased the pay for any staff members, including myself, since I started. If we don't do this, we might lose some of them, and I think they're too valuable to be replaced easily."

"If we don't do this, will we lose you as well?" Dennis, the treasurer, cut in. He was shrewd and saw the implications of what she was saying.

"I'm not looking for another job, if that's what you mean," Linda answered smoothly. She'd been expecting that question, and it was true: she wasn't actively looking. "But I think you would find, based on my research, that if I did leave—if I took a new job or if I was hit by a bus or whatever you want to call it— the board would need to advertise the position at least at the level I'm asking for here if you wanted to find someone with the experience to build on the success we've had over the last few years."

"I know you've done good work, Linda," John, the board president, said hesitantly. "But this feels like a lot of money to ask for all at once. I mean... Can we get there over two or three years?"

Linda nodded. "I understand the concern. I had it as well when I considered the budget implications. But here's my response. This is going to sound like tooting my own horn, but this is the time for it, I guess, so here goes: very few people could have brought the Historical Society from what it used to be to where it is now. It took a unique blend of fundraising, market- ing, and business sense. You can see that in our increased donor retention and major gifts program, our media coverage, and increase in revenue from the pioneer cabin. I would also add that our initiative to save the historic bell tower downtown was successful primarily because of my understanding of political advocacy and my ability to forge partnerships. This proposal brings my compensation to a level that reflects the hard work I've put into the organization to make it bloom."

"Ok, ok," John said. He'd been convinced. "What do you think, Dennis? Can we afford this?" he asked, turning his attention to the treasurer.

Dennis shrugged. "As Linda said, we're ahead of budget. There are three months of reserves. It's not like we're rolling in money, but it's certainly a workable figure. In the end, it would probably cost five or six hundred more a month. That's an expense we could manage if the board wanted to."

"Well, I'm just going to say it," Mike, the vice president, huffed. "We're a nonprofit. *Non. Profit.* And paying more than seventy grand is a lot of money. I don't want to get too personal here, but it's more than I take home and I don't work at a nonprofit. It doesn't seem like nonprofits of *any* kind should be paying so much."

Linda was about to point out the part of the proposal where she showed the salaries at other organizations like the Historical Society when Joan, the board secretary, did the work for her. "Oh, that's silly talk. I earned $70,000 when I retired ten years ago, and I didn't have half the responsibilities Linda has. Frankly this should be a no-brainer. A bargain at twice the price, as my dad used to say," Joan laughed.

Mike didn't have much to add after that. The conversation shifted to how to present it at the board meeting. Linda suddenly realized that any discussion of whether she *should* get it was behind them. Now it was just about *how* to make it happen. She was starting to feel pretty good.

"Why don't you give us a few minutes to talk on our own," the board president said toward the end.

Linda sat outside the meeting. In ten minutes, everyone but the board president left, and Linda went in to talk to him.

"We're agreed that we'll put a raise in front of the board at our next meeting," he said. "But Mike really argued hard against the full amount. We're going to recommend a flat $70,000. At that pay rate, he could support it."

It wasn't a huge reduction, but Linda was upset all the same that he'd knocked it down. Instead, she focused on the other part of what she asked. "I can understand if you want to keep it to $70,000, but in that case it's important to me that the board agrees to a two percent cost-of-living increase at the end of the year and then annually after that."

John frowned. "We forgot to talk about that part."

"This is the right thing to do. It will prevent me from falling behind again and it will be a good baseline for the whole staff to keep their pay competitive as well," Linda said.

John nodded. "All right. I think we can sell that to the full board. I'll put it on the agenda. With the four of us supporting it, I don't think you should have any problems. Congratulations."

Linda had gotten her raise, and an annual COLA to go with it.

Dealing with a "no"

Things worked out well for Linda, but what if your board turns you down flat? I'd say you have a couple options. The first is to talk one-on-one with your board president to find out why the board turned down the request. Was there a particular argument that held sway? A particular person who objected? Is there a financial fear around the raise or is there a question about your performance as the ED? These are hard questions, but if you've been turned down, I believe you deserve to know the answers.

In these situations, I recommend two things. First, thank them for their consideration of your request. Then ask for a performance and compensation review in six months to revisit the question again. It's almost impossible to turn down that request.

If there are issues the board wants you to address, six months gives you time to address them. It gives you time to build up reserves or win over skeptics on the board. The board will know you want the raise and they'll be watching you. So, make sure your Executive Director reports are thorough and do the best work you can.

Furthermore, if you've asked for the raise midyear, when you create the next budget you can make sure the budget has room for your raise. Don't put your raise in as a line item, to be clear. But if you're asking for a $5,000 raise, then you owe it to yourself to present a budget that has at least that amount in "profit." Give them the room to make it an easy call.

If even after that six-month compensation review, you can't get a raise...well, it's time to start assessing your options. If your nonprofit is healthy, if you have the money in the bank, if you've made the arguments in your favor, if you've gone through a six-month waiting period and you *still* can't get a raise, then it's not worth banging your head against the wall over. Find another board who will appreciate what you can bring to them and their organization.

Let your board miss you when you're gone.

Thoughts on benchmarks

Sometimes a board will want to approve a raise if you meet certain performance goals or benchmarks. In general, if you can avoid these, I would try.

Assessing an Executive Director is already hard for a nonprofit board. They are evaluating your performance based on their perception of how things are going and a couple meetings a month, which doesn't give them the clearest picture. So, you can understand how both a board and an ED might be tempted to tie compensation to certain agreed-upon benchmarks and metrics since it feels more concrete to them.

But it doesn't always track. If you based your compensation on the health of your nonprofit, then a recession, the passing of a major donor, or some other outside event could cause you to have a bad year financially. It's not that you can't ask for a raise in a bad year, it's just harder. Especially if you set yourself up to get a raise based on a metric that's not really under your control.

Besides that overall issue, there are two risks with benchmarks you should be aware of: The first is if your goal is too vague, reasonable people will disagree on whether it was achieved. If the goal says that the ED should "meaningfully increase fundraising" to get a raise, there could be a lot of discussion at the end of the year about what is "meaningful." Alternatively, if the goal is so specific (like, say, increasing donations from major donors from $25,000 to $40,000), it encourages the ED to be single-minded about achieving this goal, possibly to the detriment of everything else, including, perhaps, the wishes of the donor. Pushing major donors so you can get a raise is a bad look and is very shortsighted overall.

Here's the truth: the job of Executive Director is multifaceted, especially at a small nonprofit. It's a constant balance between competing interests. One day, you're meeting donors, the next you're writing a grant, and the next you're filling in behind the counter because your one employee is out sick. (Or maybe that's all on the same day!) And it's *all* important. Picking one or two or ten benchmarks and tying compensation to those benchmarks is hard in a job where defining the right work is just as important as doing the work.

Don't agree to "a percentage"

You may find a board member who says, "Why don't you just take a percentage of however much you can fundraise? That way you have an incentive to raise money."

Generally speaking, this isn't (and shouldn't be) done. In fact, the Association of Fundraising Professionals considers it unethical. It may *feel* like aligning incentives, but in fact, it pushes the ED (or whomever is raising money) to become too transactional with donors. Your rate of pay at the end of the year shouldn't depend on this. You're not a commission salesperson.

Wrapping up

As I advise you do in preparation for meetings with major donors, I always recommend rehearsing and practicing for an important conversation. Plan out how your discussion with the executive committee might go, polish your written proposal, and work on your opening line and responses to common rebuttals.

Getting a boost in pay often makes you more willing to do the work and rise to the challenge. It's not even about the money as much as it is the knowledge that your board values the work that you do. I hope you find that as well.

AFTERWORD

This work we do is vital. Whether it's for your specific community or for the world, motivated and talented nonprofit leaders are desperately needed these days. I hope this book helps to both inspire you and give you new tools and resources to bring to your organization. I sincerely hope it can help you flourish and thrive at your nonprofit.

As I said early on, it is my hope you will be able to come back to the book every so often and look for new ideas and insights that have new resonance. The act of writing it certainly made me thoughtful about my work. It was a joy to reflect on my experience at nonprofits both large and small as I outlined and wrote this book.

Thank you for allowing me to spend this time with you.

The remainder of the book is comprised by three additional chapters that relate to specific scenarios—how to start as a new ED, how to be a part-time ED, and how to let go.

PART THREE
APPENDICES
(EVERYTHING THAT DIDN'T FIT IN THE REST OF THE BOOK)

covering

Your First Hundred Days at a Nonprofit
Part-time Job, Full-Time Leader
On Letting Go

EIGHT

YOUR FIRST HUNDRED DAYS AT A NONPROFIT

IN HIS FIRST one hundred days as President of the United States, Franklin Delano Roosevelt accomplished so much that every president since then has attempted to do the same. With each new president, there are tons of articles written evaluating how "the first hundred days" went.

One of the reasons that the first hundred days are so important—for a president and for the Executive Director of a small nonprofit—is because there is a sort of honeymoon effect. There's simply no baggage yet. Over time, relationships between an ED and a board can calcify. The past informs the future, in other words. If a particular board member doesn't like how a certain decision was handled, you might find that she is less inclined to support the next initiative or that you need to slow the process down to find common ground again. Or, after the early days, a board member might come to believe you represent "too much change" and approach every new proposal with a high degree of scrutiny. These kinds of scenarios can happen over time. But at the beginning, it's much less likely to be the case. Everyone is still thinking ahead to your *potential* and they aren't lingering on your mistakes (because there hasn't been time to make too many yet!).

That gets to another reason for the honeymoon effect. Problems that arise early in your tenure are probably not your fault! They could be the result of lingering issues from the previous leadership that are now coming to a head, or simply caused by something getting missed during the transition from the old ED to the new one. No one's fault, necessarily, but it's now on your plate. EDs don't usually get blamed for these because it's clear to the board that they didn't cause the problem. So you get to look good because you're the one with ideas on how to clean up the mess, not the one causing it. This dynamic also helps create a sort of halo around you in your first few months.

(Before we start, I should point out one final thing—there's nothing magic about one hundred days. It's just over three months. So it's long enough to get meaningful things to happen but also short enough that it's a useful frame for "the beginning" of your tenure as the ED.)

So let's get your new job started on the right foot.

Before you start

There's a lot you can do for your nonprofit before you even walk in the door. Here are some good first steps:

Ask for short bios (and maybe even pictures!) of staff and board members.

You're going to have to get to know people soon, so why not get started with a better idea of the people you will be working for and with. If there are more than three employees, you may want to ask a board member to draw an org chart for you too if one isn't on paper (it rarely is—or needs to be—at a small nonprofit but in the early days, it will help you picture how everyone relates together).

Ask for as many operational documents as possible.

This can include bylaws, board policies, current budget compared to actuals, last year's budget compared to actuals, an employee handbook, strategic plans, annual reports, vision statements...basically anything that will help you have a solid understanding of the organization *before* you start.

Ask to fill out employment forms in advance.

New employees usually need to fill out tax forms, contracts, payroll forms, and other documents. Try to get these done in advance if possible. If not, schedule an hour with the appropriate staff member or board member to go through them on your first day. (I will have a lot more on the first day's schedule in a moment!)

Ask for your email address and tech accounts to be set up before you start, if possible.

Once you've accepted the job, there shouldn't be an issue with this. You're in! It's possible though that some might quibble and say "Well, you're not getting paid yet," or "You're not working for us yet." But this information can at least be set up for you in advance and then a day or two before you start, you should be able to get access. You don't want to waste your first day trying to get technology wrangled.

Ask for a donor list, with giving levels if it's available.

You might know some of the donors already, in which case you can reach out and share the good news about your new job before you start. Or, if they aren't familiar, getting this list of donors will help you be ready for your first day and week, where you can call or email the organization's top donors right off the bat. Again, there may be valid reasons people want to wait until you're actually a paid employee before giving you this information. If that's the case, then hopefully it can be waiting for you in the office on day one.

The goal of getting some of this done in advance is to preserve as much of your first day as possible for meeting people and not filling out forms. Let's move on to that big day!

Your first day

Ok, it's your first day on the job. What's your focus?

Wake up early, eat a good breakfast, and put on your gameday outfit. You don't have to look like a Wall Street banker. But this is a day you may want to dress just a little nicer than you might on a random Tuesday.

Your overriding goal for the day is primarily to get to know the people. That's why I recommend trying to get all the forms handled in advance. It's possible that your first day's schedule will be drafted by the board president, but if you see a lot of HR and time for filling out forms, you can and should push back and ask to get that done in advance. But many EDs may need to figure out how to fill their first day on their own. I *highly* recommend that you sketch out a plan in advance. It will feel much better than winging it. Here are some productive things you can do on your first day:

. . .

Ask for a tour.

Get oriented! Even if you've been in the space before, you likely don't know where everything is. Have someone show you around—from the coffee maker to the storage closet, it's good to know the lay of the land.

Ask staff to have short one-on-one sessions with you.

Fifteen to thirty minutes each is probably enough. These meetings are a chance to get to know the staff and their work. Keep them light. You're not grilling anyone. Focus on building the relationship.

Have breakfast or lunch with your board president or the full executive committee.

Carve out space for a meal with your new boss or bosses. Ask questions, answer questions, and get to know the people you will be working for. This would also be a good time to propose a weekly, or every other week, standing coffee meeting or lunch with your board president.

Address your new staff as a group.

Even if this isn't on your calendar, you might be called upon to do this, so be prepared to speak. The basic message is this: "I'm so excited to be here. You've built a great organization. I'm excited to join the team. Here's why I love this work and a little more about me. I'm happy to get to know each of you better soon." *Don't* talk about change. You're going to be delivering a lot of change, probably in ways that you don't even realize, simply because you're you and not the last ED. But *talking* about change in your first introduction is going to get everyone worried. Even if you have a new staff hungry for a change, it's best to *show* them the changes you want to make later, not just vaguely tell them about it on your first introduction.

Plan the rest of your week.

We'll get to "your first week" shortly but if you have your email address set up in advance, make time to send out emails to board members, top donors, or key partners. Invite them to meet you for coffee or schedule a call. People who hear from you on your first day on the job will notice and appreciate it!

Read.

Yes, it's ok to read on your first day. If your morning is jam-packed with meeting people, it's ok to take some time in your office to look at all the documents you've been given. If you're an introvert, it is especially the case that you'll want this time.

Unpack.

Make your office your own with photos, calendars, art, and other office supplies.

Here's an example of how a first day schedule might unfold:

8:30—Arrive
8:45—Tour and brief introductions to staff
9:00—Address staff
9:30—One-on-one meetings
11:30—Working lunch with the board president
1:00—Get computer set up and technology sorted

1:30—Read and review donor data

2:00—Email donors and board members and schedule appointments or calls

3:00—Unpack office and get settled, with an open door to staff who want to bring you questions or ideas

5:30—Day one, complete!

Your first week

Now that your first day is under your belt, it's off to the races. Here are some things you'll want to accomplish in the days that follow:

A staff meeting.

You need to get caught up to speed! No matter what the "normal" staff meeting schedule is, you should try to get one on the books within a week of starting. Elsewhere I recommend starting staff meetings with a request for stories—meaningful examples of how the nonprofit's services affect real people. So you can start the meeting with that. It's a good way to hear about what a nonprofit is doing without just getting a lot of reports.

Later in the meeting, staff members can share some highlights about what they're working on and where they could use support from others. These kinds of report-focused meetings can get dry if you try to use them too frequently. But to get up to speed on what's happening at the nonprofit, it's a decent way to start.

Pick up the phone.

Some people hate talking on the phone and some people

love it. I used to love long calls—I spent hours on the phone talking to friends. But now I feel like I have to steel myself up for a call. It's just not my thing. I'd rather text someone or meet them in person. But during this first week especially, picking up the phone and calling your biggest donors is a good use of your time.

Often, office workers are accustomed to using email to schedule calls with other office workers. This may not be necessary when trying to reach a donor. In these cases, especially when you are introducing yourself, a call may be your best bet. The reasoning—if you reach them, great! You get to have a nice chat. But if you don't, a sunny message letting them know you called will make them feel just as good. Emails will never have that kind of cache.

So pick up the phone and get to know people. Ask them how they got involved with the nonprofit. What do they love about it? What are their stories? If it feels like it's a good connection, then invite them to meet up in person and keep the relationship going.

Get caught up with the finances and the budget.

This should be a high priority—high enough to include in your first week on the job. What is the state of the finances? You should have meetings with both your bookkeeper and your treasurer. If you are uncertain about your ability to understand a balance sheet or a profit and loss statement, then meet with these two separately. Ask a lot of questions to your bookkeeper and then you'll be more informed when you meet with your treasurer.

With your bookkeeper, you'll want to go through what each line item represents, how expenses and income are processed, and how you can generate reports when you need them. Then generate the reports.

With your treasurer, you'll want to know how the board approached the budget, whether there are any stretch goals, and whether there's a "can't miss" piece of the budget—as in, the fundraiser *has* to get to a certain threshold, or a grant *has* to be successful, to make the entire budget pencil. You can probably figure these things out on your own with time, but your treasurer (in theory) knows the budget better than anyone currently at the nonprofit, and should be able to highlight these areas for you.

In addition, use the information in the earlier chapter on money and on my website http://bit.ly/LBONLbonuses to run a cash flow report as soon as you can. You'll want to know this early because the results may determine how the first one hundred days go for you. Do you have to worry about each dollar coming in and out of the organization? Or is there room for you to focus on other things?

Knowing this is vitally important. When I started as ED of City Club of Tacoma, I discovered that there was so little money in the bank that I would struggle to pay myself in the first month. That's not a good place to start! But I was able to move quickly and work on membership renewals right out of the gate to get some money in the door. If I hadn't looked for it, it would have caught me off guard and *that* would have been a disaster.

Your first decision.

It's bound to happen, but at some point this week, someone will ask you to do your job. Heaven forbid! A staff member or board member will bring something to you and ask for a decision. And it's certainly possible that it will be about a topic or issue that is wholly new to you. But you're the boss now. So, what to do?

Here are some questions to ask the person who brought you the issue:

- Can you catch me up on the backstory?
- How did the organization handle things like this before?
- What's the benefit of changing as you see it? The downside?
- Who is this going to affect?
- What do you recommend?

It's perfectly fine not to make a snap decision in the moment. But if the decision has low financial stakes, you might just want to use this as an opportunity to practice deciding something! It's also an opportunity to back up a staff member. When you know which way you're leaning, asking your staff member what she recommends will give you insight into her decision-making process. If they match up, then backing her up by going with her recommendation is a good way to start that relationship. (And if they don't match up, you can ask more questions and figure out where you're both coming from.)

Doing your job when you don't know what it is yet.

You will have more and more of these moments as you go. You'll be asked to do your job while you are getting your feet under you. If the nonprofit is in a field you're already familiar with, you'll have a leg up here. But even if that's the case, there will still be places where you are called to make a decision where you aren't sure what the right course is. Follow the model above and seek information. Assess the risks and ask your staff what they recommend. You certainly don't have to listen to them every time. You are, after all, the boss. But when you're uncertain, getting this kind of feedback will help you with your own decision-making.

If the decision you're facing has higher financial or reputational stakes than you are comfortable taking on this early, use the framework in the bonus chapter on managing change at http://bit.ly/LBONLbonuses to plan your actions: Assess the issue, look for the root problem, visualize different paths to success, and take the safest possible first step. And call your board president!

Your first month

Let's move on to your first month. You're doing the work and you're finding your groove. What should be your focus?

"Never eat alone."

In his book *Never Eat Alone*, Keith Ferrazzi makes a compelling case that leaders, as well as folks in sales or development, should, well...never eat alone. Basically, the theory goes—sharing a meal is *incredibly* relational and it's a great way to get to know people and form real bonds with others that will be valuable later.

In the Pacific Northwest, where I'm from, this often means lunches and coffee appointments. In the South, which is much more hospitality-oriented, this might mean hosting meals in your home or dining at a donor's home. And sometimes it depends on the kind of people you are working with. Some folks will want to meet you at 6:00 a.m. to get in nine holes on the golf course before work. Others will want to do drinks at 4:30 p.m. And others will prefer going for a walk and chatting while you do. The point stands—meetings are rarely the best way to get to know people. But get a stack of pancakes between you and a real relationship will develop.

Now, most small nonprofits can't afford the meals budget this theory suggests. But *especially* in your first month at a nonprofit, you should be looking to have a lot of time with donors, board members, and stakeholders, and these kinds of "out of office" meetings are an appropriate way to do it.

Meet every board member one-on-one.

You might not be able to get everyone scheduled before the first board meeting. But give it a try. You work for these board members! Get to know them early. How did they find the organization? Any special memories there? What inspired them to join the board? What visions do they want to see happen? Treat them as you would a donor and a boss—because they are a bit of both.

Share of yourself and who you are, but I'd keep the focus on the board members.

Write a really great Executive Director's report.

At some point, you'll have your first board meeting as the Executive Director. And a really good way to start that meeting is to write an amazing Executive Director's report. At http://bit.ly/LBONLbonuses, I've included samples of actual reports I've submitted to different boards over the years, if you'd like some inspiration. Usually you can use a few paragraphs to highlight key things you want the board to know and then a series of bullets of "other actions" or something like that.

For this first report, however, you might want to be more effusive. So in addition to the first few paragraphs, consider having very detailed notes here. You might have a document open on your computer and add to it every day. And then consolidate. So if you have a list of donors you've met with, then combine it into a single bullet. Writing "Conducted initial cultivation calls with twenty-three major donors" looks really good! Especially if there are many other equally great bullet points around it.

Plan to address the board.

Whether you want to or not, you should plan to address the board at the first board meeting. Because it's almost certain that your board president or someone else on the board will say "Maybe you can update us on how the first month has gone" at the meeting. So plan ahead.

The goal of this, like the ED report, is to reassure the board that they made the right choice: You're *on it*. Everything is going really well. You have a bunch of ideas and things you're excited to implement. You're building relationships with staff and you're even more excited to be on the team as you get to know people.

In these situations, I often choose three specific areas to talk about. More than that, and things get muddy. Less than that, and it feels incomplete. Your ED report is a good start for the areas you want to touch on.

Finally, I strongly advise against saying anything negative in this report, especially about one of the core areas of the nonprofit—mission, people, or money. It's going to get a board member either very defensive or very curious, and it's too early for you to do much about it anyway. Of course, there are probably some issues you've seen by this point. But addressing them, or even alluding to them, at this moment—when you don't have much trust built up yet and when you might be new enough you're misreading the situation—is too early.

Now, if you have discovered *serious* issues in your first month that really should go to the board as soon as possible, then I would inform the executive committee before the meeting about the problems and talk about courses of action. Then, together, you can decide how much of what you've found should go to the full board. But this first presentation is more of an introduction than it is business as usual.

Your remaining one hundred days

Let's wrap up "the beginning" of your tenure. During the remaining couple of months, you will begin to see the initial sprouts of any seeds you've planted, and you will hopefully be able to plan even larger projects. Here are some things to keep in mind as you really get a handle on what it takes to steer this ship:

Who do you already know?

In the first month or two, a lot of the work of the nonprofit is getting to know the board, staff, volunteers, donors, and partners of a nonprofit. But as time goes, you should also look for ways to bring people you already know into the world of the nonprofit. Your friends, family, and loose network of acquaintances want to know about the work that you are so passionate about. It may turn out that some of them are actually as passionate about it as you are! You won't know until you reach out.

So look for early ways to engage your circle with your nonprofit. Post on social media about what you're doing. Invite people to join you at events. Give friends and family a private tour. You bring something to the nonprofit besides yourself—

you bring your connections. Don't forget to introduce them to your new nonprofit and share that side of yourself.

Now, this can feel risky to some people. After all, you are a fundraiser. Some of your friends might be afraid that you're going to ask them for money. And you might be afraid that they will think that, so you just don't invite them. But don't let that stop you. At this stage, it would be way too soon to ask anyone for money. You are simply sharing of yourself.

For those who seem interested, invite them to come to your organization's fundraising events. You should always feel comfortable inviting people to these events. It's an ask, yes, but it's a soft ask, and it's easy for someone to decline by citing a real (or fake) scheduling conflict. It's water under the bridge if they say no. But for those who come, who give, who connect, they start to become donors as well as friends. And that's ok. It's good! They want to give and support the organization and you shouldn't hide from that. But for everyone else—your friends who worried that you were going to ask—you're never going to get to that point because they will self-select out. Don't sweat it.

Working with someone else's budget.

During the first few months you're going to have to get a handle on someone else's budget. As I said earlier, the first thing to understand is cash flow—how much money is coming in and how much is going out. That's vital in the early days. But after that, you're going to start finding that you and your predecessor have different ideas about where money should be spent. You might identify that marketing is a key priority—but you're working with a budget of $100. Does that mean you're constrained to spending only $100? Or maybe you find yourself in the reverse position—there's $10,000 in the marketing budget and you have no idea how on earth you could spend that much. Do you have to spend it anyway?

In both cases the answer is no. My advice is this: *don't worry too much about the budget and spend the money how you want to spend it, so long as the total expenses don't go over budget.* Does that surprise you? Coming from the person who told you that budgets are a form of board policy? That budgets are vitally important and all that?

You and your predecessor are different people. It's as simple as that. You can't shackle yourself to a budget that you didn't write.

The board almost certainly won't care either. *If...*

Yes, there's an if. Here's how to have a free hand when you approach a new budget:

- *Seek to understand first.* If there's a line item that seems too large or too small than how you would spend the money, ask around. Staff or board might know more about why it's set up the way it is. You can also go to the books for research. Look at the prior year's budget and the prior year's actuals. You may learn whether something happened that caused the new budget figure.
- *Look for trade-offs.* If you really want to spend $1,000 on marketing, but have only $100 in the budget, then you need to find $900 somewhere else in the budget where you can save that money. That's the true key to having a board sign off on differences in the budget. So long as you don't go over the total budgeted expenses, you should have a lot of leeway from the board on where you are spending.
- *Talk to the treasurer or the finance committee as*

expenses happen (or in advance for the bigger items you vary from the budget). If a board member sees that you went $900 over your $100 marketing budget, they might worry that you are spending indiscriminately. But point to where you intend to find the $900 when you present the numbers and it will go much more smoothly.

- *For the big stuff, put it in next year's budget.* For the largest of changes, you may need to defer them until the next year's budget. Perhaps it's because the expense is tied to a new revenue idea you have, or some other big change you intend to implement. In those cases, prepare the board in advance through the budgeting process. Unless you are in a dire emergency, don't add a major new expense into a budget unless you absolutely have to. And then, again, that's when you really need to present to the board and explain the situation and propose your plan of action.

Weighing one big change versus steady leadership.

There are two basic strategies for approaching the first one hundred days—swing for the fences with a big change or try to change nothing. Your approach will be informed by the state of the organization.

There are some good reasons why you might want to be cautious and implement a "change nothing" approach. If the few months preceding your tenure have been tumultuous, you might choose the steady leadership approach. Or, if you are new to a field or you have a lot to learn about the organization or the clientele itself, then extra caution is warranted.

I'm inspired by the model of a pastor I know who entered a church that was deeply divided and had many contentious factions. He was very clear—I'm not going to make any changes for a year. He worked one-on-one with church council members and parishioners and tried to heal those divisions. But he was true to his word. Almost nothing changed during that first year.

I have to be upfront—this goes against my nature. But what I saw gave me a new appreciation for the slow and steady approach. So if the organization has been through turbulence and strife, a steady hand on the tiller with no major shakeups is a workable strategy if you have the patience to deliver on it.

But if you are craving the chance to start a transformative process, or if the last ED was in the seat for a decade, or if everything feels like it's in a rut, then launching a big change initiative is a good strategy. Choose one area of the nonprofit and make that a focus of your work. You can do a lot in one hundred days if you push yourself and push the organization. Leave everything else virtually the same, but see if you can make change happen there. (Again, use the bonus chapter on change for a solid approach.)

The "honeymoon effect" means that some people may be more willing to go along with change early. And you can establish early on that you have a big vision and a big agenda. So if this sounds like you, go for it.

A final reflection

After a hundred days on the job, you're *in*. You know the work much better than you did at the beginning, and you're (hopefully) getting real traction on key projects. I think this is a perfect moment to take a bit of time, even a half day, and reflect on how you did and what you need to do next. What went well? What mistakes did you make? What still needs to be addressed?

What new and interesting projects could really create a lot of good?

I find this kind of reflection really helpful on a personal level. It informs my decision-making and helps me keep my eye on the ball and not get distracted by the small stuff.

Some of this may form the bones of a report to the board—a sort of extended ED report about where you are and where you're going. Or it might inform some added context at a board retreat. Setting aside this kind of time to reflect and plan will make all your work that much more effective.

Iterate

What comes after the first one hundred days? The *next* one hundred days, of course. String a few of these hundred-day spans together and after a while you should start to see real differences from the time you started.

As you grow into the job, you will start embarking on projects and initiatives that take longer than this time frame. That's almost assured because big things usually require a lot of time and energy.

That said, it's easy to lose your way when projects take that long. So if you ever need a kick in the pants, get out a calendar and mark off one hundred days. Treat it like a sprint—something you do every so often with some rest afterward—and try to finish a big project before the hundred days are over. You'll be amazed at what you can pull off.

NINE

PART-TIME JOB, FULL-TIME LEADER

IT'S common at very small nonprofits to have a part-time Executive Director. Doing the work of a nonprofit at half time—or even quarter time—is challenging, but doable. And I've been there. During my three years as Executive Director of City Club of Tacoma, I was part-time. I had a range of other jobs to make it work. For some of it, I was working with my wife to build a small business that helped nonprofits with marketing and communications. I also served in elected office while I was at City Club, meaning that I was holding down three jobs (ED of City Club, the business with my wife, and elected office). We also welcomed our first child during my time at City Club and I ran for office during that time too. So I think it's safe to say I know what it's like to have a part-time ED role while balancing a ton of other obligations.

Let's dive into the challenges of running an organization part-time for these very small nonprofits.

Part-time hours, part-time pay, full-time responsibility

How does a nonprofit Executive Director lead an organization with ten to twenty hours a week? Answer: she probably can't. There's simply too much work to do the job properly. And I want to be clear—many EDs working forty hours a week (or more) feel some of this too. There's always something more to do. But, with planning, focus, and discernment, a full-time ED can figure out how best to structure her work to get the most important parts done in that amount of time. That may not be possible for a part-time person.

So what choice does she have? The first choice is obvious: she works more hours than she's paid for. This is blatantly unfair, of course. But it's common (and I did it too). There are several reasons an ED might do this. For one, a nonprofit needs certain things to happen in order to simply have its doors open. And if those things can't be done in the time an ED is paid, she might choose to work more to make sure it happens. That could be because of a commitment to the mission or the realization that if she can't keep the doors open, then she's out of even her part-time job.

Another reason a part-time ED might work more than she's paid is that she wants to build the organization into one that *can* pay her more. Founding EDs are a little bit more likely to do this than other kinds of EDs, but I've seen it work both ways. An ED translates her fierce commitment to the organization into fundraising and earned revenue and eventually builds up a full-time job for herself. This takes grit and determination and a real "long game" strategy from the ED. But it can work.

Before you put in extra hours as a part-time ED, you have to consider what your ultimate goal is. What's keeping you there—the money, paltry though it may be? The love of the mission? A way to stay connected to your community? Get very clear.

Because at some point you may open your paycheck and realize with a sinking feeling that you've just spent countless hours all in service of a few hundred dollars. Once you start to feel that you could be earning more—that the trade-off isn't worth it—it's hard to squash that feeling.

So what's the alternative to working more than you're paid?

The first option is extreme delegation. Volunteers—both board members and regular volunteers—might be needed to pick up the slack. (My section in "People" on working with volunteers will help a lot here.) This turns the ED into a field marshal, deploying her troops to a variety of small tasks. This is plenty of work on its own to juggle, but it may also allow an ED to carve out the time she needs for the most important aspects of her job.

At City Club we had a communications committee that helped us with marketing and such. One member wrote press releases. Another handled Twitter. Another wrote the newsletter. They were a volunteer committee that supported me and worked with me. As a part-time ED, they were helpful to have.

There are a lot of benefits to this kind of delegation approach, but it does have some risks and downsides. It may invite the board into operations, which complicates the relationship with them. It increases the likelihood of mistakes or miscommunication.

To use another example from City Club, one time I discovered that a small board committee had met (without me) to review credit card payment processing options. I didn't ask for this and actually found it to be pretty unhelpful. I was using an option that was fast and easy for me, which was a priority given my limited hours. Changing to a more cumbersome system would be more work and the savings between three percent and two and a half percent were so minimal that, in my opinion, it wasn't worth it. So I was resistant to the change and made it clear I was upset that they were interfering with operations. The board members were caught off guard and even hurt by my pushback. (I remember one said specifically that she was trying to tackle this for the organization because I was part-time and they didn't want it on my plate.) I was frustrated that they were interfering in operations and—in the end—gave me more work, not less. And in their eyes, they were only trying to help and I got mad at them for it. It left a bad taste in everyone's mouth.

So, before you start down the road of leveraging board volunteers, I recommend a little pre-work with your board about the ways that a board member can volunteer for operations. You, the ED, are in charge of operations. When board members volunteer for operations, in those moments they are reporting to you. If they are accustomed to being "your boss" at the board meeting, this can be awkward. It's best to ask your board president or the executive committee to make this clear to the rest of the board early.

Another alternative to working yourself to the bone is to simply leave big things undone. I know, that sounds like sacrilege. But sometimes it might be the only course. If you don't think you can reasonably get to something and you don't think you can delegate it, then you owe it to yourself to ask, "Would the world end if I didn't do this thing?"

Of course, if they could be left undone, then they must not have been that important, right? Maybe that's true. But when everything is screaming "Pay attention to me!" it's hard to discern this right off the bat. So a little time asking yourself whether something can be delayed or skipped outright might bring some clarity. As long as it's a conscious choice to put something aside, and not just something you forget about, you should feel ok about using this strategy when appropriate.

Finally, a part-time ED who is tech-savvy will find more success than one trying to do it all by hand. There are many services out there that can help an ED run a lean and mean organization. Many of these have free or low-cost levels that would be perfect for a small nonprofit. Lean into technology as best as you can and let it do a lot of the work for you.

Even given those alternatives, you likely *are* going to have to work more hours than you're paid for...at least sometimes. If the nonprofit has some seasonality in the schedule, you might be able to take it easy when crunch time is over and make it all pan out. But there will be weeks that take a lot of hours (such as before an event or around board meetings) that might bump you over. It's just bound to happen.

But, unless you are deeply committed to the work (or deeply committed to building the position into a full-time salary for yourself), I don't think you should be working *excessive* hours over your pay. The board should not expect it of you and you should not expect it of yourself. It's unfair to you and—if it never changes—it hurts the nonprofit in the long run. Because unless you can actually build the salary pretty quickly, you run the risk of burning out and finding a job that pays you closer to what you're worth.

Do your best to keep your hours reasonable.

The balancing act

Ok, so we talked about the first big difficulty of being a part-time ED: figuring out how to get the work done. Now let's talk about the second big difficulty. If you're not getting paid for full-time work...you probably still need money from somewhere else!

If you have a spouse or partner who is bringing home enough money, maybe you can afford to earn part-time income. If not, you are going to have to balance having two or more jobs.

The obvious conflict is scheduling, such as when a board meeting and an obligation for another job are scheduled at the same time. Plan well in advance and make sure your board is aware that sometimes you may have to juggle commitments. But this can usually be managed.

The real difficulty is when the ED's needs diverge from the needs of the nonprofit.

For a full-time salaried employee, this is pretty rare. But it's much more common when the ED is part-time and earns their money from another source. I'll give you a couple examples of the kinds of situations that might happen.

Let's say a part-time ED makes money on the side building websites. Everything is going well until she meets someone who could be a major donor for her nonprofit, or who could also be a major web client. When she shakes that person's hand, what job does she lead with? Does she talk about her great web design skills? Or the nonprofit she runs?

Or consider an ED whose primary job is in city government and is an ED on the side. What does she do when she is confronted with a decision in her "day job" that will adversely affect the nonprofit? Or perhaps the reverse is even more problematic—what if there's an opportunity to steer city funding to her own nonprofit? Should she do it?

Another example: an ED with a side job in consulting with other nonprofits. When another ED who runs a partner nonprofit calls her up to ask for help, is she helping for free in her capacity as a partner, or is this an opportunity for paid work?

These are difficult questions and, I hate to say it, there is not always a clear answer. But I can offer some advice to help navigate these waters.

The first is that you should be scrupulous whenever possible. Remember what I said in the first chapter about "reputation management" for your nonprofit. The Warren Buffett quote was this: "Lose money for the firm and I will be understanding.

Lose a shred of reputation for the firm and I will be ruthless." I wrote this about your nonprofit, but it is true for yourself as well. In the long run, you'll do better to choose the scrupulous route. Your reputation at both the nonprofit and your other job will improve.

Second, let's talk about the situations where you meet someone who could be a donor for your nonprofit or a client in your other business. In general, look for ways to let the person take the lead. You might introduce yourself with, "I wear a couple hats, actually. I'm the ED of a nonprofit dedicated to early childhood learning and I design websites too." The prospective donor/client will ask more about whichever part of your job she's most interested in.

The important thing to know in this situation is that delivering on one side of your job will help you make inroads for the other sides of your job. A donor who loves working with you because you handled the cultivation, ask, and stewardship process with care is much more likely to use you for that website she needs. Design a great website with prompt communications and professionalism and you'll be in a good place to share more about your nonprofit. So, the question of "client or donor" is a false choice. If you handle the relationship well, you might get both the client and the donor.

Focus on the relational side of your job with your board and the nonprofit's stakeholders. Earn their trust and these possible conflicts won't seem like such a big deal to anyone who knows and trusts you.

Going full-time

If your dream is to eventually work your way into a full-time ED role at the organization, you owe it to yourself to communicate that to the board. Usually this can be done through your executive committee or through an annual review process. You might also get it into a three-year strategic plan to have a full-time Executive Director, and everyone knows that you want to be that leader.

But they won't know this is your goal if you don't tell them. If you bring in an extra $10,000 in fundraising, and the board is discussing ways to hire a coordinator or invest it in some other way that does not increase your compensation, you are setting yourself up to be disappointed and upset. They need to know this is what you want. And you need to hear them express their willingness and agreement too. Maybe some board members think a part-time ED is just fine and would rather put the money elsewhere. That's useful information for you to know now! So sort this out early. You owe it to the board to tell them this is your goal. And, if they agree, they owe it to you to say (in some form) that they will work toward that goal as well.

If that's *not* your dream, that's ok too! It's fine to be a part-time ED if that works for you. It allows you to invest back into the organization and set up a later ED for future growth.

How to grow

Ok, so we've addressed the two big conflicts that a part-time nonprofit ED will have in her position and you've gotten some clarity as to whether you want to grow with the nonprofit. But how to actually grow? In an earlier chapter, I list the Four Ds of growth—documentation, database, development, and determination. All of those apply to a very small nonprofit with a part-time ED, and I encourage you to review those again.

But there are some special circumstances for a very small nonprofit. Even small dollars are meaningful. Consider a nonprofit with a $50,000 annual budget. Through a sustained effort to build monthly donors, it adds $1,000 a month in new income. That's an additional $12,000, giving them a budget of $62,000. A twenty-four percent increase in funds from one year to the next. That's huge. It's much easier for a very small nonprofit to grow this quickly. (A nonprofit with a million dollars in annual revenue would have to add $240,000 in a single year to grow by twenty-four percent. It's hard to grow that fast when you're that big.)

So how to grow as a very small nonprofit? It's a balance between what I think of as the "one big leap" approach and the "go slow to go fast" philosophy.

"One big leap"

Sometimes you need to grind away at a big goal to make progress. You put everything else aside and just...*work*. A massive grant application takes forty to eighty hours, but when it comes up in your favor you've doubled, or tripled, or quadrupled your budget. Or you put a huge amount of effort into your annual fundraiser to take it from $5,000 net to $25,000.

For a small nonprofit, these big wins can be both exhilarating on a personal level and incredibly meaningful in terms of the budget. They take the organization to a new plateau from which to work. There's a real difference being an organization with a $20,000 annual budget and one with an $80,000 budget. And sometimes a lot of hard work on a couple key areas will get you there.

The downside of this approach is that a nonprofit can suddenly get a bunch of cash it doesn't really know how to spend. Because there was a single-minded focus on finances, nonprofits pursuing this route can find that they spend a long time trying to "backfill" on the business of the organization. "Oh yeah, we need a treasurer" or "Oh yeah, I guess we should have a policy for that" can dog an organization like this for a long time.

Because the maturity of the nonprofit hasn't caught up to the finances, so to speak, the organization may end up squandering its financial windfall. This is where the Four Ds come into play.

"Go slow to go fast"

The other approach is to lay the groundwork for later success operationally and organizationally. This is methodical and relational. It doesn't look for a "lottery ticket" to get the nonprofit to the next level, but rather focuses on building organizational maturity before financial security. You do everything right. You pass all the policies you should have (and then some), you have engaged board members, you have the capacity of a much larger organization than you actually are. And because you're doing it right, the money follows. People gravitate to success. Fundraising, partnerships, and reputation all increase modestly year over year. Five years of ten percent increases across the board can have a real effect.

But it's not all rosy. The downside of this approach is simple: money is really nice, and the longer a nonprofit is "very small" the longer it remains fragile and susceptible to outside shocks. And, without real funds, the organization may struggle to actually fulfill its mission, even in a limited way. Board members might leave the nonprofit because "all we do is talk" or it feels like the organization is never making any progress.

How to balance these goals

You do need to do both. Just pursuing one approach won't work.

Trying to make a big leap is a really good idea! When you're a very small nonprofit, it doesn't actually take that much new money to make a real difference. So keep a strong focus on fundraising and try to climb to the next plateau.

Delegate where you can, but this needs your attention. If your nonprofit has a budget less than $100,000, then an annual appeal that brings in an extra $5,000 even has the potential to make a real difference. Every dollar for a very small nonprofit is meaningful in that sense.

But you also can't skimp on the organizational side of this!

Put a lot of work into board development.

One of the temptations for a part-time ED is to focus on the work and leave the board to their own devices. This means not going to committee meetings, entirely turning over fundraising to them, and not working with the board on budgets or policies. It's the wrong approach. For one, at a small nonprofit, everyone needs to be rowing in the same direction. And that won't work if you're disengaged. And second, the board truly does have the power to augment the work you're doing. Fundraising is most powerful when an ED runs point and leverages the relationships of the board, to pick just one example.

Board work is slow work. It's painstaking. It's messy. But it's good work. And investing your time in board work will pay off for you and the organization in the long run.

Program, fundraising, board

That means that you're going to have to plant your two feet in three squares—program (as in, what you actually do), fundraising, and board work. It's quite a dance!

Look for those big wins, but also put a fair amount of energy into the organizational capacity and maturity of the nonprofit. While, of course, actually doing the work. It's definitely hard.

But that's the work for the ED of a small nonprofit if you want the nonprofit to flourish in the long run.

Partner, partner, partner

As you're doing this dance, here's a practical tip that should help: partner with other organizations. A very small nonprofit can often find real power in partnerships. You can take your mission to the next level by working with other nonprofits, governments, and more. The logic is simple: you don't have to create everything from scratch.

This can be helpful in terms of "back end" expertise where you benefit from the experience and resources of larger organizations. It can also be helpful in terms of audience and marketing. If you are trying to provide services to teenagers, it's often much easier to find an organization (like a school or the YMCA) that is willing to partner with you. If you have an expertise that is outside the other organization's expertise, you might be able to really make some magic happen. One plus one is three.

I consulted with one very small nonprofit about rebooting their board. And as I got to know the nonprofit, I grew impressed with their partnerships. This very small nonprofit teaches creative writing to youth, especially "at-risk" youth. They've partnered with the local juvenile detention center to run a book club, the parks district to offer classes through the district, local museums and bookstores, after-school programs in the school, and more. They have their own events and classes too. But having these partnerships expands their services far outside what they would have had the capacity to deliver on their own.

Early growth

When the nonprofit starts growing, you're going to be faced with a hard choice about where to invest your additional resources. You could ask the board to pay you for more hours. You could sink it back into the organization's mission. You could add a part-time staff member to take some of the smallest tasks off your plate to free you up for bigger work.

Where should the new resources go?

At first, I think the key question to ask yourself is this: What could I do with this money that will reduce the chance that I burn out in a few months' time? Maybe that means a small raise for you so that you feel valued and can let go of your other job. Maybe it means hiring a coordinator to staff the registration table at events and handle those little details so you can fundraise more (or just take a vacation once in a while). Or maybe you're not in danger of burnout right now and are happy to reinvest the funds into the work.

Only you know the right answer. Because what we need to avoid more than anything is burning out the ED of a very small nonprofit. If the ED leaves suddenly or she loses her heart for the job, the organization is suddenly at massive risk.

Later growth

As the nonprofit continues to grow, the two best places to invest those gains are into your program and further fundraising. Program, because this is the reason for your existence, and the better you serve your community the more you will attract new dollars. And fundraising, because you can't continue to grow without building these resources. You might invest in fundraising by hiring a coordinator to help in the office or an event manager to throw the fundraiser. Or, counterintuitively, you might invest in fundraising by hiring someone in program so that *you* can do more fundraising. Yes, that counts too!

Lean and mean

In those early days, every dollar counts. So use them wisely and try not to invest in something because of *optics*. We all do this to a certain extent. "Oh, no one will take us seriously if we don't have...[fill in the blank]." But most of the time, whatever you finish that sentence with isn't true.

Instead of an office, can you use a coworking space or work from home? Instead of hiring a bookkeeper, can you use an online service? Instead of a custom website, can you use a template with a low monthly fee? Instead of renting a room for board meetings, can you meet in someone's home?

In the early days, it's worth it to question every expense.

Until it's not

At some point, a small nonprofit will have to invest in the important things. You can't keep an organization together with duct tape forever. Use the tools throughout the rest of the book to build your nonprofit and grow out of the "very small" phase.

TEN

ON LETTING GO

THE LONGER AN EXECUTIVE Director stays at a nonprofit, the more the job can fit like an old shoe. You can really sink into the position. The years will add depth and experience and the organization will mature. But unless you intend to die in your chair, at some point you are going to have to say goodbye.

Let's start walking you through the process of letting go.

It's ok to leave

Maybe this is obvious and maybe it's not, but I think we should start here. It's ok to leave your job. You are allowed to retire. You are allowed to find a new job. You are allowed to go work in a big corporation and make three times the money you did at the small nonprofit. You aren't chained to your nonprofit. If you need someone's blessing, you have mine.

If you are starting to think that the job is becoming "same old, same old," or that the mission doesn't light a fire in you the way it used to, then don't feel guilty about leaving. It's ok.

Are you growing?

If you are wrestling with whether you want to stay or go, my question to you is this: Are you growing? I'm not asking if you're happy. Jobs are one possible reason why we may be happy at any given point, but certainly not the only one. But if you reframe it this way—"Are you growing?"—I think it's a more clarifying question about your job.

If you're not growing, you should consider what you could do to change that. There might be new opportunities you can create for yourself at your current organization that will light that fire again. Or things might just feel played out for you. It might be someone else's turn.

Leaving can be scary

There are many reasons why nonprofit EDs are hesitant to leave. One ED might be worried that the entire ship will fall apart as soon as it loses its captain. Another might fear that the nonprofit will become unrecognizably different under new leadership. And *every* ED considering leaving their job will worry about how the organization will fare without them. Even if just a little bit.

These fears are totally natural, but they shouldn't be enough to stop an ED from moving forward. In almost all cases, the feared outcome can be addressed and managed.

That said, sometimes an ED's fears can become barriers to moving forward with the leadership transition. In some cases, there may be *unstated* reasons that are often even more personal than the ones already mentioned. For example, an ED planning to leave doesn't always know where the next job will come from. That can be scary and cause some reluctance on her part to go forward.

As another example, an ED might be subconsciously worried about a change in *status*. We don't talk about status much in our culture, but I felt the loss of status particularly hard during one job transition. When I left a job managing a nonprofit, my next job was in the development office of a much larger organization. I got a pay increase and the work was for an organization I cared about, but the status change was difficult to manage on a personal level. I went from being (in my mind) "a somebody" who was quoted in the paper and publicly recognized for my work to (again, in my mind) being a cog in a much larger machine. It was a difficult transition. EDs who are stepping down from a job—or more commonly retiring—often see this status change coming and it can make them anxious long before they actually retire.

Similarly, an Executive Director may be reluctant to leave their nonprofit because the job has become tied up in her identity of herself. She *is* her job and her organization, and stepping down feels like she will lose something important about herself.

These kinds of personal fears about leaving the job are real and they are valid. In fact, I'd go so far as to say that coping with them can be a true grieving process. In our society, we often only associate grief with death, and that makes us reluctant to put the word next to something as supposedly mundane as leaving a job or retiring. But because we aren't willing to name it as such—but perhaps feel the loss just as keenly—the effects can be emotionally traumatic and can cause us to act in ways that we otherwise wouldn't.

So if these feelings go unaddressed in an ED, they can hold back the organization that she loves. As I said, I've felt these questions of status and identity. I've felt the grief over losing parts of my identity. They are hard feelings to grapple with. I am grateful to have found a therapist to help me through them.

EDs who are struggling here may find success with that approach as well.

What are the risks to the nonprofit if the ED leaves?

One of the most common fears that can keep an ED at a nonprofit is the fear that everything will fall apart when she steps away. It's safe to say that, most of the time, nonprofits don't collapse when there's a leadership transition. But there are potential issues that can emerge. When an ED leaves her job, here are the biggest risks facing the organization:

- Relationships with key donors or partners may change, wither, or cease entirely.
- The quality of the nonprofit's services or program may be reduced as the new ED "gets up to speed."
- Staff, volunteers, or board members find themselves in conflict in a way that didn't happen under the previous ED.
- In short, important things will get missed.

These can and do materialize during a change of leadership. Even during the best leadership transition, a donor might feel overlooked or a certain aspect of the nonprofit might be lessened. Almost always, though, it's not life or death for the organization. With planning, all of these fears are *manageable*.

What are the benefits to the nonprofit if the ED leaves?

But there's a counter to this as well.

There are actual benefits to the organization that can come with a change in leadership. Even if you are a rock star Executive Director, there may be benefits to the organization. Sometimes a nonprofit can calcify under an ED. Things fall into a routine and a familiar pattern that—even if they are effective routines and patterns—can start to feel like going through the motions. Or the underlying reasons for the system might change, but the nonprofit doesn't adapt with the times. Slowly, the nonprofit becomes less responsive than it once was. New leadership can break through that.

New leadership can also bring new relationships to the organization, or new talents and skills. You might have been amazing at getting the nonprofit off the ground and on its feet. But what if the next ED really knows how to run a capital campaign or has tight connections with local funders?

So if you're afraid of what the nonprofit will lose when you leave, don't forget about the potential gains they could make with the next leader.

Preparing an organization to survive without you

Whether you are actually planning to leave the job or not, there is still great value in preparing the organization to survive without you.

In many ways, it's what I've been advocating for since the first chapter. Remember how early on I said that you should try to extricate yourself from day-to-day operations of the nonprofit? Or when I advocated for focusing on documentation and databases as part of the Four Ds? Those are good operational goals because they help you better lead the organization. But they also are good preparation in case you get hit by the proverbial bus (or decide it's time to take a new position and further your career elsewhere).

For a year or so during my time at City Club, I was the half-time Executive Director with no employees. I did everything. This time also happened to be when my wife and I were expecting our first child. About two months before our daughter's due date, I delivered to the board a very detailed document about the steps that needed to happen to pull off a City Club event on the off chance I would be unavailable that particular night. From passwords, to name tags, to timelines, to lists of people to call, I documented a key portion of my job. Had our daughter arrived earlier than expected, we would have been ready.

Creating these kinds of documents can be laborious. You may not need to get as detailed as I did if you don't have imminent plans to leave. Look at the "Four Ds" section again at the end of the first chapter for some ideas of documents that will be helpful in the future. At the very least, you can write a series of one-page briefs for major topics. Each might have different needs, but that's ok. A one-page overview with a timeline for the fundraiser would be really beneficial. The mission of the nonprofit could be divided into sections with a page for each program. Reconciling the books at the end of the month might be a step-by-step guide with screenshots. Whatever makes sense and doesn't take you too long to create.

Contextually, it might help to think about these as documenting your process more than teaching the next ED what to do. As I've said, everyone brings their own skills and experience. How you do something isn't necessarily how the next person will do it. But it still may be useful for them to understand how *you* went about your job.

Sharing the load

Sometimes EDs will discover that nothing happens without their express say-so. No matter the hierarchy or the size, culturally speaking, the ED is the final decision maker on *everything*. The board turns to her for its most major decisions. Or the staff is reluctant to step up and take responsibility without the green light. In a very small nonprofit, this might be workable. But eventually the organization will need to grow out of it. And this is *especially* true if the ED is planning to leave.

As the old saying goes, give a child a fish and they will eat for a day. But teach a staff to make decisions for themselves and they will be able to serve the nonprofit when you're no longer ED. (That *is* how it goes, right?)

If everything—even the tiniest detail—is run by you for approval, you will have to retrain your staff and board. For example, you might bring key decisions and policies to the board and present two to three paths and ask them to help you determine the right course of action. (I discuss this early in Chapter 6 when I talk about inviting the board into your brain.)

For the staff, look at how the ED in the appendix on the first hundred days uses the power of questions to elicit a recommended course of action from staff members. Encourage them and back them up instead of overruling them. Sometimes if they have it mostly right, and not *totally* right, you might have to let experience teach them how to get it mostly right instead of correcting them the rest of the way. Do this more regularly and use staff meetings to help your team share their expertise among themselves. "Tanya, you had an interesting experience at the front desk last week. I thought you handled that upset member really well. Can you lay out for everyone what happened and how you handled it?"

The more a board can step up to the job, the more staff can be empowered to make decisions, the more an organization can thrive without you at the center of it.

These changes are best made slowly but with persistence. It's nothing different than what I encourage throughout the rest of the book. But now you're doing it for a different reason: to help make sure that the nonprofit has the skills and the muscle memory to go about the work when you're gone.

————

If you follow everything in this book, you should be able to step away with reasonable confidence that the organization will continue. There's nothing certain anywhere in life. So I can't one hundred percent promise you that it will all be ok. But if you can build a decent board, regular cash flow, diverse revenue sources, and the ability to serve the public in a useful way, it's a good bet that you can successfully pass the baton. Use the Four Ds! Document your relationships. Use a database. Develop the skills of your staff and board. And use your determination to build a cash reserve to provide a cushion for the next ED, should the nonprofit need one.

An actual transition

Once you've decided you are ready to leave, the next step is to plan your transition. How this goes really depends on your next job.

Are you retiring?

In this case, I'd recommend giving at least six months' notice. That should be ample time for the board to get ready and find a replacement. Since there's no complication with you taking a new position, it's a little clearer cut. You also might consider planning an extended vacation after you've retired. So if you give six months notice, what if in seven months you head out in an RV to see as many national parks as you can? This gives you something to look forward to and it also forces the board to actually hire a replacement. They can't ask you for a few more months if you're planning to be in Yellowstone.

Are you looking to be the ED of another nonprofit but don't have a job lined up yet?

The best practice in this scenario is to give your board *a lot* of notice, maybe even a full year. This makes it easier for you to openly look for a job without feeling like you're doing it on the sly. You are banking on the connections you've made, your network, and maybe your knowledge of what's happening with EDs of other nonprofits to find your next position within that year. Finding an ED job can take a long time and there may not be any openings early on, so the year gives you some time to both ready your current nonprofit and find the next job. Most likely, this news isn't "public" information outside of the board or a small group of staff. Work out a timeline to inform key donors and partners a month or so before the public announcement. (That announcement probably comes six months before you leave, when a search process begins.)

Are you looking to be the ED of another nonprofit and have already found your next job?

If you have been applying for ED jobs without telling your current board, and have been accepted for one of those jobs, you now need to figure out how much notice you can afford to give. I've already said that it's common for Executive Directors of nonprofits to give several months of notice to their board. But it's also common to accept a new position that won't actually start for several months too. So you should feel reasonably comfortable that you can ask your new nonprofit if you can start in, say, three months' time. That transition will ask a lot of your board—three months is a fast search process—but it's doable.

What if your next job is something other than being the ED of a nonprofit?

If an ED accepts a new ED position but won't start for three to six months, that's a reasonable transition. But that length of time for almost any other job won't fly. Often, they want you now, and they're willing to wait a few weeks *at most*. They might be willing to negotiate, but not by much. If you've given your board early notice, and worked to prepare the nonprofit for your absence, you should be able to feel confident leaving fairly suddenly toward the end. There might be a gap in leadership at the nonprofit between you and the next ED, but with planning in advance, it should be manageable.

Two weeks isn't enough

Please, though, do whatever you can to avoid giving just two or four weeks' notice. It is a huge shock to the nonprofit to leave that suddenly. If you're leaving *any* professional job, two weeks' notice is the bare minimum you should give. Giving such short notice as an ED is even worse. You may as well have been hit by a bus for as much preparation as you're able to do in that amount of time.

If, for whatever reason, you need to leave your job so suddenly, you owe it to the nonprofit to do what you can to make this work. Help them find an Interim Executive Director who can fill in for a few months (I've served as an Interim ED twice and there are usually a handful of retired EDs who may be willing to do this kind of work). Or recommend a particular employee stepping into the role for a short period of time—with you promising daily or three times a week check-ins with that employee.

But however it shakes out, it's hard on a nonprofit, so try to avoid this if you can.

Supporting the board during a transition

In the early weeks or months of giving notice, you should be a willing partner to help come up with a transition plan. You can help with a calendar and detail work. As I've said in other contexts in this book, boards are better at decisions and individuals are better at *tasks*. So you can help with those tasks, such as posting the position on job boards or other administrative tasks that actually help the transition take place. (I do have a sample timeline for a transition later in this section.)

Also, share your documentation with them. Let them ask questions and ask for more. Report on the database, policies, and the state of the nonprofit. The board may be scared about what's getting missed. You can help show them that you are preparing.

As the board gets their feet under them, you should slowly step back from the transition process. Help them with details and information, but leave more and more of the decisions to them. You're leaving, and they are making the hiring decision! You don't get a vote anymore.

ED to ED

At some point the nonprofit will extend an offer to someone new. Now the transition becomes a handoff. The details of it will depend on your skillset and the skillset of the incoming ED.

You should be prepared to pass off your documentation at this point. I also think it's a kindness to offer to get email, phone, passwords, and such arranged in advance. Perhaps you could order a box of new business cards, so the incoming ED doesn't have to wait weeks for that.

I also believe you will want a series of one-on-one meetings together. The new ED should take the lead on what she wants or expects, but I think at least a couple meetings before actually starting the job is a good idea. Be honest about the state of things, answer questions, and share what you know. It will be appreciated.

Overlap

Sometimes a nonprofit will intentionally have their Executive Directors overlap in the office for a couple days, a week, or sometimes even longer. The longest I've seen was a couple months.

My *personal* bias is that there be no overlap. It's expensive to pay two EDs at the same time. And it may create some awkward scenarios about who is actually in charge. For the incoming ED, it may also feel like she's just shadowing somebody around for hours on end, like her schedule is not her own, and like she's waiting for the old ED to clear out so her job can actually start. I prefer documentation to hands-on training because of this sense of inertness.

That said, if there is an overlap, I think a day or two is probably fine. You, the departing ED, may want to relay some key information about complex systems that don't transcribe well to paper. Or perhaps there are other relational things you can do together like meeting some of your biggest donors. But anything longer than that, and I believe it creates a frustrating holding pattern.

Answering questions after you're gone

A better way to serve the new ED is to be willing to meet for coffee or answer the phone when she has questions, even after you've moved on. For example, you could schedule a meeting for two weeks after the new ED starts and answer any new questions. At the end of the meeting, offer to meet again or reiterate that you can answer questions via phone or email.

This is unpaid work. But I think it's a kindness. And it puts the new ED in the driver seat. If she wants to reach out, she can. If she doesn't, that's fine too.

I would also recommend limiting contact with the board or staff members. Churches have very strict rules about this when they switch pastors and they help keep everyone focused on the new leader. I think it's a good model. So if someone reaches out, just redirect them to the ED. This is not a permanent ban. But give it a few months before you start socializing again with the board and staff of your former nonprofit.

Sample transition timeline

Here's an example of a transition timeline with some of the key things that have to happen. This is over the course of a year. If you can't do it that fast, work to get as many of these steps to happen as you can.

June—Announce to the board that you are stepping down by June of next year.
July through September—Document what you can and do whatever you can to help leave the nonprofit in a solid place. If you are looking for a job, you may want to start having lunches around your community and seeing what you can learn about

what's happening in the ED world. Trusted friends can know you're leaving but not many others.

October through December—Support the board with job descriptions, operational overviews, and other information they will need for a job search. Keep up with your network about other job openings.

January—Tell major donors, partners, staff, and any other key stakeholders that you're leaving. (Gut check: if you haven't found *any* leads at all for a new job yet, you might consider post-poning this for a couple months. But now that you've made your intentions known to the board, you're going to have to leave at some point. You can buy yourself two to three months' extra time, but maybe not a lot more.)

February—The organization emails about your departure and the job is posted. Hopefully you've found some jobs to apply for at this point.

March and April—Support the board during the search process. They might need logistical support on interviews or have ques-tions for you. You'll also be working to manage staff. Hopefully, you too have some interviews lined up.

May—The new ED is announced. You start working to support the new hire and also preparing for your new role, hopefully.

June—The transition is complete.

July and August—Answer questions if the new ED has them.

It's possible that you won't find a job before you actually leave and it's possible that you will find one within six months instead of one year. It changes the timeline, but the rough order of the steps should stay the same.

A note to founders

The founder of a nonprofit will almost always have a harder time stepping away than other EDs. After all, this nonprofit would not exist without you! So it's understandable why, at a very basic level, founders might believe that it won't exist without them going into the future too.

This might sound odd at first, but I have a strong belief that nonprofits exist mostly so that founders *can* leave. My logic goes like this: If an idea doesn't need to last after the founder leaves, then it didn't need to be its own nonprofit in the first place. Instead, it could have been just a service or ministry of that individual to the community. It could have been the program of another organization. But if the idea is compelling enough to get individuals donating, foundations making grants, and people joining the board, *then it's a good enough idea that it should live beyond the founder.*

And that means, founders, that your goal is to build something that doesn't need you anymore.

In that context, there are a couple of things I want counsel founders in particular. The first is to warn you that it will be tempting to move to the board from your role as ED. There are some benefits to the nonprofit if you do this, but also some real downsides. One of those downsides is that some potential well-qualified EDs won't apply for your job when it opens because they will believe that they will be micromanaged by you. You might swear up and down that you won't do this, but even if that's true, the perception will still likely be there.

Another downside is that you may trap yourself on the board, likely in the role of president. It's "natural" for the founder to become board president. And founders usually go above and beyond in their work for the nonprofit. Everyone else on the board will look at the job that the founder is doing and think, "I don't want to be board president—it's too much work!" Thus, the founder stays president until she burns out (this is especially difficult on her if she left her job as ED because she was burnt out there).

So be very cautious about joining the board. If you want to help, tell the new ED that she can call you for anything, anytime. Leave it up to her. Ask for big projects to spearhead. Even if you still do hours of work every week for the organization, it's better than doing it while also serving on the board. Doing it *from the outside* means you are reporting to the ED (not the other way around). And you are letting the board flex their own muscles without you.

But even then, consider taking a month or two off after you leave. Check in, make sure that the new ED knows you are available to answer any questions. But give yourself that time to see how it goes without the nonprofit in your day-to-day life. You might find there's room for something new and even more exciting.

Actually letting go

At some point you will have to let go of the nonprofit in your heart.

This can be difficult. Mostly it takes time. I'd avoid getting too far wrapped into whatever's happening at the nonprofit. Don't inquire about board members or whether a certain issue has been dealt with. Let questions come to you. If you want to help, serve the new ED and keep the rest of your contacts at the nonprofit to a minimum.

Intentionally schedule things you like to do when you used to have board meetings. If you used to meet on the first Wednesdays of the month, make sure to intentionally claim that night back. Plan to go out to dinner for a few first Wednesdays or have some friends over. Do it until you catch yourself forgetting that the board is meeting without you.

I'm reminded of a story my friend Kristen Corning Bedford tells in her book *A Generous Heart: Changing the World through Feminist Philanthropy*. She talks about how she stepped away from a nonprofit she cofounded. And then, when she came back years later to attend a fundraiser for the organization, no one there knew she was the cofounder. She was just another donor there to show her support.

She found a sort of beauty in that, and I do as well. It's really nice to be celebrated *when you leave a job*. But you don't need to be celebrated years later.

I wasn't the founder of the Grand Cinema, but I was a leader during a pivotal time in its history. But when I go to the Grand Cinema these days, I'm just there for a movie and some popcorn. That was unimaginable to me in the year or two after I left. But it turns out, it's rather liberating. I've moved on, and so has the Grand.

WAS THIS BOOK HELPFUL TO YOU?

Please considering leaving a review online to help other small
nonprofit managers find this resource as well!

Also by Erik Hanberg

*The Little Book of Gold: Fundraising for Small (and Very Small)
Nonprofits*

*The Little Book of Boards: A Board Member's Handbook for Small
(and Very Small) Nonprofits*

*The Little Book of Likes: Social Media for Small (and Very Small)
Nonprofits*

CONSULTING AND SPEAKING

I've traveled across the country facilitating board retreats and working with nonprofits of all sizes. I've also spoken at several nonprofit events and conferences about fundraising, nonprofit leaderships, marketing, boards, and much more.

If after reading this book or my others, you think I'd be a good fit for your nonprofit or association and want to learn more you can find more at ForSmallNonprofits.com.

You can also sign up here to receive more information from Erik Hanberg about all facets of small nonprofit management: http://bit.ly/forsmallnonprofitsemail

ABOUT THE AUTHOR

Erik Hanberg is an expert in nonprofit management, fundraising, marketing, and leadership. His books for nonprofits have sold more than 20,000 copies.

He has served as the director of two nonprofits, the interim executive director of two more, and served in positions in marketing and fundraising. He has been on more than twelve boards. In addition, he has consulted with nonprofit boards and staff of dozens and dozens of nonprofits and foundations across the country.

He has served for twelve years as an elected official on the Metro Parks Board of Tacoma, a junior municipality with an annual operating budget of $50+ million.

He lives in Tacoma, Washington, with his wife and two children. In addition to his nonprofit writing, he also has several novels, and even a play or two.

————

Find him online at:
    https://www.forsmallnonprofits.com
    https://www.erikhanberg.com
    or on Twitter at @erikhanberg.

ACKNOWLEDGMENTS

I owe a lot of people gratitude for their help making this book possible. Starting with my family, first and foremost. My parents modeled board service and giving back and I am deeply grateful for their example. I also need to share my appreciation for my wife Mary. In addition to encouraging me to write this book (and all the others) she has been a partner in everything I do. Not just in life and family but business as well, when we ran a marketing company together for many years that was focused on supporting nonprofits. And, of course, she has designed the book covers for all my "little books."

I especially want to thank the early readers of this book as well. My friend and fellow author Kristen Corning Bedford. Along with Allison Sing, Funmi Akinyele, Jill Blakeney, Susan Willats, Wendy Burtner, Emily Prior, Bri Fairley, and Kevin O'Connell.

I also am grateful to Beth Attwood and Cindy Jewkes for their professional editing of this manuscript. If there are still typos and missed words, it's not for a lack of review on their part.

And, finally, I want to thank the tens of thousands of readers who have purchased one of these books over the years. I am honored that you turned to me when you needed ideas on improving your nonprofit and I hope these slim volumes were of some help.

Knowing that my readership was interested in my books pushed me forward, made me a more keen observer, and made me better at my own work. Thank you.

The Little Book of Nonprofit Leadership
An Executive Director's Handbook for Small (and Very Small) Nonprofits
Published by Side x Side Publishing
Copyright © Erik Hanberg 2021

Cover by Mary Holste
Cover photo by Ingrid Barrantine

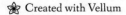 Created with Vellum

Made in United States
Troutdale, OR
12/07/2024